DATA ENGINEERING AND AI FOR BEGINNERS

REVOLUTIONIZING DATA PROCESSING AND ANALYTICS BY LEVERAGING ARTIFICIAL INTELLIGENCE FOR EFFICIENT INPUT COLLECTION, STORAGE, AND TRANSFORMATION

WILLIAM LEESON

VWORKS PUBLISHING

CONTENTS

PART II
ADVANCED TECHNIQUES IN DATA ENGINEERING

PART III
ADVANCED APPLICATIONS AND FUTURE PERSPECTIVES

YOUR FREE BONUS

As a way of saying thanks for your purchase, I'm offering for FREE to my readers:

- 1 ebook "*ChatGPT Chronicles- A Quick Guide to Mastering Health, Wealth and Wisdom with Artificial Intelligence*"
- 2 video courses on ChatGPT (Beginner & Masterclass)
- 40,000 useful prompts to save you countless hours of work

To get instant access just go to:

https://vworkspublishing.com/ChatGPT-free-bonus

With this, you will be able to automate thousands of tasks in your daily work that includes:

- Writing emails
- Crafting effective resumes
- Designing marketing plans
- Brainstorming Ads creatives
- Learning a language
- Getting organic traffic
- Turbocharging your social media channels
- Expanding YouTube outreach
- And much, much more!

Scan for Free Bonus

INTRODUCTION

In a world fueled by data, the potential for transformative change is undeniable. Many captivating possibilities, like a healthcare system that predicts outbreaks by analyzing subtle shifts in patient data are not just the stuff of science fiction but are becoming a reality through the convergence of Data Engineering and Artificial Intelligence (AI).

As a data engineer dedicated to transforming raw data into actionable insights, I used to be stressed a lot. As an engineer, though I love what I do, it was a process that constantly tried my patience as I had to balance accuracy, efficiency, and scalability while negotiating the complexity of data collection, storage, and transformation.

This is the world where data engineers live – battling mazes of data pipelines, navigating storage solutions, and decoding the cryptic languages of transformation. Of course, being a data engineer has its own rewards, but we all wish we can make do without the stress.

So, walk with me to uncover how the amalgamation of AI and data engineering can simplify, accelerate, and enhance your data processing and analytics endeavors.

You will gain a full understanding of how to apply AI to automate your data engineering processes after reading this book. You'll learn cutting-edge tactics to overcome difficulties that, up until now, seemed to go hand in hand with data engineering. And learn how AI can be used to improve storage alternatives, streamline data pipelines, and fine-tune transformation procedures.

You'll embark on an engaging journey that investigates the complexities of data engineering and the transformational potential of AI within these pages. Prepare to understand the mysteries of effective data collection methods while making sure your inputs are thorough and accurate. Explore the world of data storage thoroughly to identify solutions that are adaptable, safe, and appropriate for your specific needs. Additionally, data transformation will become less mysterious, giving you the ability to edit and polish your data with unmatched accuracy.

As a seasoned data engineer and AI enthusiast with a history of assisting others in establishing themselves in this sector. I am in an ideal position to guide you through this revolutionary journey since I have a ton of practical knowledge and a burning desire to bridge the gap between data engineering and AI.

Are you ready to transcend the limitations of traditional data engineering? Do you yearn to wield the potent amalgamation of AI and data prowess? This book is not just an offering of knowledge; it's your ticket to a world where data becomes more than ones and zeros. It's a world where insights are not just gained but unlocked, where problems are not just solved but anticipated, and where data engineering and AI converge to shape the future.

Join me in the pages ahead and embark on a quest that promises to revolutionize your understanding of data engineering and AI. Let's journey together, shaping the future with every line of code, every insight gained, and every transformation achieved.

PART I

FOUNDATIONS OF DATA ENGINEERING AND AI

I remember when I first started my data engineering journey – as much as I loved processing data, making it readily available for analysis and ready to tell a story,I didn't like the data cleaning part. In fact, I always couldn't wait to be done and over with it. Setting up pipelines, coding, and scripting was what I signed up for, not checking for outliers or filing in empty values.

But then came AI tools, and they made my work lots easier. Now I can just focus on processing the data, while it does the mundane tasks of collecting, validating, cleaning, and integrating data effectively. And let's not talk about the evolution of data storage while ensuring security and privacy. I must say, AI made a lot of processes a breeze.

1

INTRODUCTION TO DATA ENGINEERING AND AI

Although data science has always been at the forefront of data and technology, recent trends show that data engineering is becoming just as, if not more, valuable. Data drives decision-making and innovation in any organization, regardless of niche or sector (Fenwick *et al.*, 2009). Whether in retail, healthcare, banking, or engineering, data has shown to be a vital asset. But, since data is only information, how is this information translated into useful insights? You got it right with data engineering. You know how vital the backstage crew of a great theater show is; they're always working behind the scenes, invisible but crucial to providing a faultless performance - data engineering is the same way.

What is Data Engineering?

The process of gathering, storing, and transforming data typically falls under the responsibility of data engineers. Similar to the backstage crew behind a theater production, data engineers lay down the foundation behind the scenes enabling scientists and data analysts to perform their magic. They act as a link between data and complex knowledge (Pitt *et al.*, 2003).

Although each discipline has its role in the world of data, data engineering, and data science are two fields that collaborate to convert raw data into actionable insights. Data engineering involves converting information into formats. This includes tasks such as collecting, cleaning, integrating, and modeling the data to create datasets that can be utilized for machine learning and other analytical applications (Nagafabadi *et al.*, 2015). To ensure that the generated insights are based on quality and suitable information, close collaboration between data engineers, scientists, and other stakeholders is crucial.

Scientists utilize methods and learning algorithms to extract valuable information from the available dataset. Thanks to frameworks and pipelines developed by data engineers these professionals can efficiently access, prepare and process the information, with ease (Diaz *et al.*, 2021).

The role of a data engineer typically involves the responsibility of collecting data from sources such as databases, APIs, and sensors. Their primary task is to ensure the gathering and inputting of data into the system (Carbone *et al.*, 2015). As you may already know, each piece of collected data needs to be stored. Therefore the engineer must carefully choose the storage locations based on factors, like the volume and type of data as well as any access restrictions that may apply.

And to ensure that the data is clean, there is the need to set up checks and validations to easily identify and rectify all anomalies. Engineers then set up pipelines to process the data using code and scripting to create various components, making sure that these pipelines and systems enable scalability so that the infrastructure built up can grow along with the data as it grows

(Lin *et al.,* 2013). Most times, as data engineers we have to put security measures in place to safeguard the data, especially if it's sensitive info.

Becoming a Data Engineer

I can tell you assuredly that being a data engineer is a fun experience and totally worth it. Because this process will have you at the edge of your seat, bubbling with excitement especially if like me you love solving puzzles and creating order out of chaos - I mean, who doesn't?

We data engineers also collaborate with other stakeholders, both technical and non-technical teams. This means you also need to be an effective communicator and have team spirit if you're going to yield excellent results.

So, as you can see, data engineering is that invisible hand that ensures data flows seamlessly, enabling organizations to harness the power of AI and analytics.

The Role of AI in Data Engineering

Data engineering is an ever-evolving field and follows technology right behind, adapting and growing with technology. As a data engineer, I've seen that if you want to stay on top of developments and be useful in the field of data and AI, you must constantly be open to learning new things and developing your skills.

Consider AI as a dependable partner who collaborates with data engineers to advance their field. By assisting with time-consuming processes like data preparation, cleansing, and modeling, AI makes things better (Capgemini, 2019). We can now fully concentrate on the creative and strategic aspects of our job since these time-consuming tasks are no longer on our plates. We may direct our efforts toward building ingenious data pipelines and revealing the intriguing narratives buried inside the data. It's similar to having a trustworthy partner who does the grunt work while you guide the ship toward creative answers.

AI is more than just an assistant—it's a transformational force (Daffodil Software, 2022). The automation that AI brings to data engineering isn't just about efficiency; it's about empowering data engineers to explore uncharted territories. Freed from the shackles of repetitive tasks, they can dive into developing fresh data products and services that drive business growth. Not only that, but AI's ability to detect and correct errors (a crucial part of data processing) enhances data quality, which has a direct impact on decision-making (Janssen *et al.*, 2020). It's like having a partner who not only helps you with daily work but also offers you the ability to foresee a better future.

Let's look at the intriguing perspective of AI's role as an augmenter, not a replacement (Sinsense, 2022). Think of AI as a wise mentor, guiding data engineers through their journey. By automating data cleaning and preparation, AI liberates these professionals to focus on the big picture, designing and implementing data pipelines that lay the foundation for insightful discoveries (Ghazal *et al.*, 2021). It's a dynamic partnership that enriches the field, as AI assists in unraveling complex datasets and extracting meaningful insights. The result? A powerful synergy between human expertise and AI prowess culminates in smarter strategies and more informed choices.

Imagine the efficiency of AI-driven data preparation, meticulously organizing information for analysis. This innovation isn't just about speed; it's about accuracy and precision, ensuring data engineers have trustworthy foundations to work with. AI's anomaly-detection skills deserve a mention too. With its watchful eye, AI can uncover anomalies in data, providing businesses with a safety net.

AI's power isn't confined to automation; it extends to insight generation. AI uncovers patterns and trends by combing through enormous information that could otherwise go undiscovered (Berger *et al.,* 2004). It doesn't just provide charts and graphs, but it provides organizations with actionable insights that will guide them in the right direction. Furthermore, the personal touch of AI is palpable in its knack for personalization. Think about tailored recommendations, spot-on product suggestions, and advertisements that genuinely resonate. AI doesn't just crunch numbers; it understands human preferences and behaviors.

AI's influence on data engineering is transformative. It's like having a companion that lightens the load, increases data quality, and opens the road for better decisions. Rather than advancing technology, this coalition seeks to maximize human potential. So, as AI and data engineers join hands, we embark on a future full of possibilities, where innovation knows no bounds.

The Impact of AI on Data Engineering and Analytics

Have you ever marveled at the power that is technology and its potential to transform the landscape of data processing and analytics? I, for one, have seen firsthand the incredible influence that AI is having on this ever-changing profession. AI has altered the world of advanced analytics, leaving an everlasting mark on how we process and extract insights from massive datasets. The capabilities of AI extend far beyond mere automation; they encompass a paradigm shift that's transforming the very essence of data analysis (Biztory, n.d.). By harnessing AI's remarkable ability to process and analyze copious amounts of data with exceptional speed and efficiency, analysts are now empowered to focus on higher-level strategies that fuel innovation and growth.

One can't overlook the profound implications of AI's intervention in the laborious realm of data processing. I remember sifting through many rows of data by hand, my eyes drooping over as I looked for patterns. Now, AI algorithms do the heavy lifting, spotting trends and anomalies with lightning speed. This newfound agility allows us to respond and adapt more quickly, turning raw data into actionable insights before you can say "Jack Robinson." Traditionally time-consuming tasks, which analysts would painstakingly undertake, are now swiftly automated through sophisticated AI techniques (Biztory, n.d.). The profound significance lies in liberating human capacity from mundane data cleaning and preparation, allowing experts to channel their energies into exploring uncharted territories of insights and possibilities (Data Science Central, n.d.).

AI's prowess in data analysis transcends the boundaries of human capability. The intricacies that lie within vast datasets are no longer daunting; AI algorithms have a knack for identifying correlations and complex patterns that often remain hidden from human perception (Biztory, n.d.). I recall a project where AI algorithms revealed unexpected correlations within the data, leading to a groundbreaking discovery. It felt like having a co-pilot on a treasure hunt, as we unraveled insights that were previously buried beneath layers of information. These revelations, born from AI's analytical acumen, do not merely present insights but fundamentally alter decision-making processes. This predictive power arms businesses with insights that extend beyond the present, offering glimpses into the future and rendering decisions more precise and strategic (Data Science Central, n.d.).

The synergy of AI and analytics has proved itself a game-changer. The traditional reliance on intuition and gut feelings has evolved into a data-driven revolution (Vanguard X, n.d.). In today's dynamic business landscape, AI doesn't just augment decision-making; it radically amplifies it. Imagine a world where spotting trends and patterns is as instinctive as breathing. AI's data analytics capabilities are not limited to retrospection; they peer into the horizon, identifying new opportunities and assessing potential risks. Moreover, this duo excels in enhancing customer experience and proactively unearthing fraud and anomalies in financial realms (Vanguard X, n.d.).

The symbiotic relationship between AI and advanced analytics has ushered us into an era of unprecedented possibilities. The capabilities of AI go beyond automation, venturing into the realm of insightful pattern recognition and accurate prediction (Burgess, 2018). This transformation transcends traditional decision-making, ushering in a new era where data reigns supreme, propelling businesses toward strategic excellence and informed innovation.

Exploring the Potential of AI in Revolutionizing Data Engineering

AI has limitless possibilities in today's tech-driven environment. It's not just about increasing efficiency; it's about altering entire sectors. One area where AI's potential shines brightly is in data engineering. We'll go deep into the dynamic interplay between data engineering and AI, revealing the amazing ways in which AI is transforming the landscape of data processing and analysis.

The Synergy of Data Engineering and AI

Picture yourself as a data engineer, tasked with taming vast oceans of raw data (well you're preparing to be one or one already, so that should be easy). Now, introduce AI, your trusted ally in this epic journey. Together, data engineering and AI forge a symbiotic partnership, revolutionizing how we extract, store, and transform data. AI brings automation, predictive power, and pattern recognition, enhancing the efficiency and depth of data-driven decision-making (Sarker, 2021).

AI-Powered Data Collection

Bid farewell to manual data collection, for AI has emerged as the beacon of efficiency. Imagine AI-driven bots traversing the digital landscape, gathering data from diverse sources, and meticulously organizing it for your needs. Whether you're tracking market trends or curating content for a digital campaign, AI streamlines the data collection process, leaving you with more time to strategize and innovate.

Smart Storage and Management

Storage complexities are a thing of the past, thanks to AI's analytical prowess. By studying data usage patterns, AI optimizes storage strategies, ensuring frequently accessed data is readily available while seamlessly migrating less-used data to cost-effective solutions (Saxena *et al.*, 2016). This not only saves resources but also ensures data accessibility without compromise.

Data Transformation

Remember the arduous days of data cleaning and preparation? Tasks like data cleaning, normalization, and feature engineering are expedited through AI algorithms. They identify outliers, rectify inconsistencies, and craft new features that elevate predictive models. This means your focus shifts from wrestling with unruly data to crafting insightful narratives.

Predictive Analytics and Future Insights

The true power of AI emerges in predictive analytics. By learning from historical data, AI models unveil patterns, trends, and potential future outcomes (Pan *et al.,* 2021). Whether you're foreseeing market trends, customer preferences, or legal verdicts, AI-backed predictions empower you to make informed decisions with confidence.

Revolutionizing Marketing with AI: Harnessing Data

Shift gears, and let's dive into the world of marketing. Marketing isn't just about catchy slogans and eye-catching visuals anymore; it's about data-driven precision. In this area, AI has emerged as a game-changer, with the potential to completely transform marketing strategies and campaigns.

Think of AI as your silent observer, continuously collecting and analyzing customer behavior data. This data goldmine forms the foundation of personalized marketing campaigns. The concept is simple yet groundbreaking: understand what customers want before they even know it. If a customer browses certain products on a website, AI can swoop in and suggest similar products, increasing the chances of conversion.

At the risk of sounding like a broken record, AI's power lies in its ability to automate tasks. Remember those hours spent crafting email marketing and managing social media promotions? AI can handle these mundane tasks, freeing up marketing teams for more strategic thinking. Imagine having the bandwidth to focus on devising ingenious marketing campaigns and refining strategies that resonate with the audience.

In a nutshell, AI isn't just a digital helper; it's a transformative force in marketing (Stark, 2020). The efficiency it brings to the table translates into effectiveness and personalization. The days of generalized marketing approaches are waning; it's the era of tailor-made experiences.

The potential of AI in revolutionizing data engineering is awe-inspiring. OpenAI's strides toward AGI are opening doors to possibilities that were once confined to the realm of imagination. Whether it's automating data preparation, refining predictive models, enhancing marketing precision, or optimizing judicial processes, AI's influence is profound. It's not just about technology; it's about transforming the way we work, strategize, and make decisions.

The Role of Data Engineers in AI-driven Environments

Although AI has taken a lot off our plates and made data engineering easier, it is not a replacement for data engineers and we still have our role to play in the data ecosystem. In fact, the symbiotic relationship between data engineers and AI has opened up new frontiers in data processing and analytics. So, buckle up as we discuss the fascinating landscape of data engineering in AI-driven environments.

When you think about data engineering, you might envision an unsung hero behind the scenes, quietly orchestrating the data ballet. But let me assure you, although I likened our role to that of the backstage crew, it's far from a backstage role. As data engineers, we're the architects of the data world, constructing robust pipelines that transport, transform, and optimize data to be the fuel that powers AI's marvels.

Data engineering is more than moving data from point A to point B, it also involves understanding the unique intricacies of the data, molding it into a coherent structure, and ensuring it's primed for AI to extract its magic (Buduma *et al.*, 2022). Just like a master chef prepares ingredients before they reach the dish, we prep data before AI takes over. Remember that feeling of achievement when you perfectly organized your room? That's what we do with data, ensuring that AI can navigate through it with ease.

Our role is to translate the abstract into actionable, taking raw data and crafting it into a story that AI can read. It's a blend of art and science, where each line of code we write whispers tales of insights yet to be uncovered (MacAdams, 2015).

Imagine yourself at a bustling farmers market, surrounded by an array of vibrant produce. You handpick the ripest tomatoes, knowing just how they'll contribute to the sumptuous pasta you're planning. Similarly, data engineers select and curate data sources, intuitively understanding how each dataset will contribute to the AI-driven insights that organizations crave.

The dance between data engineers and AI is not without its moments of humor and humility. There have been times when an unexpected glitch turned into a eureka moment. It's in those instances that you realize the beauty of improvisation, just like turning a kitchen mishap into a delicious experiment. Though AI is certainly intelligent, it lacks the comprehensive knowledge of data that people possess, and it is our responsibility to ensure that data is interpreted correctly.

As we navigate the intricate landscape of data engineering in AI-driven environments, it's essential to grasp the pivotal role that data engineers play in shaping the success of modern enterprises. AI, undoubtedly a transformative force, has bestowed upon us the tools to analyze and predict trends, optimize processes, and make informed decisions like never before. Yet, AI's prowess hinges on the foundation laid by data engineers.

A seminal work by Rodríguez-Mier and Abelló emphasizes the crucial role data engineering plays in ensuring the efficiency and reliability of AI systems. They elucidate how data engineers provide the essential groundwork for AI models to produce accurate predictions and insights. This is evidence that we data engineers, who laid the groundwork for the success of the AI revolution, are its unsung heroes.

The realm of data engineering in AI-driven environments is a dynamic and indispensable one. As data engineers, we wield tools that not only facilitate the efficient flow of data but also influence the trajectory of AI-driven innovation. A complex balancing act of technical mastery, original problem-solving, and adaptability is required in our line of work (Cao, 2017). We are not just engineers; we are enablers of AI's transformative potential. Remember, in the realm of data engineering and AI, every line of code you write, every pipeline you design, is a contribution to a future shaped by insights and intelligence.

So, my fellow data engineer, you need to understand that AI is not our replacement, but rather our partner in this grand symphony of data. Let's continue to craft pipelines with finesse, dive deep into the data ocean, and collaborate with AI to reveal insights that were once hidden in plain sight.

In an era where data is often compared to oil, data engineers act as the drillers and refinery operators, extracting, purifying, and distributing this valuable resource. We create the pipelines that transport data, ensuring its quality, security, and accessibility. Without this robust foundation, the most advanced AI algorithms would be akin to high-performance cars without roads to drive on.

One of the cornerstones of data engineering is data modeling. Think of it as creating the blueprint for a building. Effective data modeling involves understanding the intricacies of the business and designing a structure that reflects these intricacies, enabling efficient data storage, retrieval, and analysis (Laguna *et al.*, 2018). This process ensures that AI algorithms are fed accurate and relevant data, thereby enhancing their predictive power and utility.

Also, the field of data engineering is rapidly changing, necessitating constant adaptation and education on the part of data engineers. We need to keep up with emerging technologies. This aligns with Lao Tzu's adage that "life is a succession of natural and spontaneous transformations. Don't resist them; that only creates sorrow. Let things flow naturally forward in whatever way they like."

In the context of AI, this means embracing innovation and facilitating its integration into existing data ecosystems. For instance, data engineers have been at the forefront of operationalizing machine learning models (Zhou *et al.*, 2017). We close the gap between data science and practical applications by deploying models into production settings, allowing businesses to make data-based decisions instantly.

As we journey through the data engineering and AI industry, we encounter an ecosystem where each element thrives symbiotically, enriching the other. AI's ability to learn, adapt, and predict hinges on the high-quality, well-structured data that data engineers provide. In turn, AI empowers data engineers to process vast amounts of data efficiently and extract valuable insights that inform business decisions.

A study by Zhang et al., highlights the role of data engineers in curating data lakes, repositories that store vast amounts of raw and processed data. These repositories are the lifeblood of AI applications, providing the fodder for training and validating models. Data engineers curate and manage these lakes, ensuring that the data is clean, accessible, and contextual, which directly impacts the quality and effectiveness of AI algorithms.

Key Challenges and Opportunities in Data Engineering with AI

Navigating the landscape of data engineering in the realm of AI presents both challenges and opportunities that beckon us to adapt, innovate, and create. We will encounter pivotal cross-roads where we must overcome hurdles while embracing the potential that AI bestows upon us.

Challenges

In the quest for effective data engineering, several challenges come to the fore. The first of these challenges is data quality (Velvetech). As you know, data must be accurate, complete, and consistent, so poor data quality can reverberate through the analytical process, leading to skewed insights and erroneous decisions that can cripple businesses. It's like building a puzzle with pieces that don't quite fit – the result is far from cohesive.

Another obstacle that data engineers face is the daunting data volume. In an age where data seems to multiply faster than rabbits, managing and processing colossal amounts of information becomes a herculean task. The data deluge demands innovative solutions to ensure efficient utilization without drowning in the digital sea.

Yet, speed is also of the essence, introducing the challenge of data velocity. As data rushes in from various sources at breakneck speed, data engineers must keep up with the relentless pace. Just as a swift river can erode even the sturdiest rocks, the constant stream of data can wear down unprepared systems.

Opportunities

Amidst these challenges lie golden opportunities that beckon us to explore uncharted territories. The scarcity of skilled data engineers is a clarion call for those with the passion to step into the spotlight. As demand far surpasses supply, those who master the art of data engineering have the chance to shine in an arena that values their expertise (Pine *et al.,* 2011).

While complexity may pose challenges, it also offers ground for growth. Data engineering's intricate web is continually evolving, inviting us to grasp new tools, frameworks, and paradigms. By embracing this evolution, we can emerge as pioneers who chart the course for data-driven success.

Yet, the regulatory environment is also a fertile landscape for innovation. As businesses navigate the labyrinth of regulations governing data, those who can ensure compliance while maintaining operational efficiency become invaluable assets. Like forging a path through a dense forest, mastering regulatory intricacies requires vision and dexterity.

Navigating the Terrain

Stepping into the data-driven era presents us with the challenges I previously illuminated. A paramount challenge is data literacy, as businesses often grapple with comprehending and interpreting data. This underscores the importance of bridging the gap between data engineers and other stakeholders, ensuring that data becomes a language understood by all.

Finding the right talent is akin to prospecting for precious gems. The demand for data scientists, engineers, and skilled professionals surges as AI continues its ascent. Yet, this challenge also represents a tremendous opportunity for individuals to step into roles that shape the digital landscape.

Security forms an unassailable fortress against the tide of data breaches. The concerns raised by Insidebigdata.com resonate deeply, as safeguarding data is crucial for financial and reputational well-being. Fortified security measures ensure that the data citadel remains secured.

In conclusion, the challenges and opportunities that intertwine in data engineering's tapestry reflect a journey of growth, innovation, and adaptation. The path ahead demands our resilience, creativity, and determination as we traverse the realms of data quality, volume, velocity, talent scarcity, complexity, regulatory compliance, data literacy, talent acquisition, and security. This dynamic interplay forms the backdrop of our narrative, as we harness AI's potential to illuminate the boundless possibilities of the data-driven world.

Takeaway

- Data engineers lay the foundation for data interpretation.
- AI doesn't mean we should be complacent, it means our work should be done more efficiently.
- As data engineers, we bridge the gap between technical and non-technical teams.

2

———

FUNDAMENTALS OF DATA ENGINEERING

Overview of Data Engineering: Concepts and Principles

As I continue to delve more into the area of data engineering, I'm fascinated by how diverse this field is. Data engineering is an ecosystem of concepts and ideas that affects the way data moves, is transformed, and aids in decision-making, it is more than just pipelines and algorithms. It involves following a set of principles that instill integrity, dependability, and scalability into each stage of the data journey. These principles form the bedrock upon which data systems are built and insights are uncovered. But first, let's unravel the key concepts that underpin the realm of data engineering.

Data Pipelines

Imagine data as the lifeblood of an organization, flowing through intricate pipelines that ensure its timely and reliable distribution. Data pipelines are the arteries and veins that connect various data sources, processing stages, and destinations (Marques *et al.,* 2021). These pipelines orchestrate the movement, transformation, and enrichment of data, ensuring it reaches its intended destination cohesively and coherently. Just as our circulatory system keeps our bodies thriving, data pipelines keep organizations pulsating with insights.

ETL: Extract, Transform, Load

ETL—three simple letters that encapsulate the magic of transforming raw data into refined insights. Extract, Transform, and Load is the process that data engineers use to transmute data from its raw form to its refined state. Data engineers extract data from various sources, apply transformations to cleanse and enrich it, and then load it into storage systems for analysis (Demirkan & Delen, 2013). This process turns raw data into a valuable resource for decision-makers.

Data Warehouses

Imagine a treasure trove where valuable insights are stored, organized, and ready to be unveiled at a moment's notice. Data warehouses are the digital equivalents of such vaults, designed to store massive amounts of structured data. These repositories serve as the foundation of analytics by offering a centralized location for data querying, analysis, and visualization. Data warehouses give organizations the ability to obtain useful insights, much as a well-organized library makes it simple to access knowledge (Damiani *et al.*, 2021).

Big Data: Volume, Variety, and Velocity

In the era of big data, the three Vs—Volume, Variety, and Velocity—define the scale and complexity of the data landscape. Volume refers to the sheer magnitude of data generated daily, from sensors, social media, and various sources. Variety encompasses diverse types of data, from structured to unstructured, text, images, and beyond. Velocity denotes the speed at which data is generated and must be processed. Data engineers masterfully harness the power of these Vs, transforming raw data into meaningful insights (Howard, 2014).

Data Lakes

Data lakes provide a storage repository for vast amounts of raw and unstructured data. In data lakes, data engineers can store data in its native format until it's needed. Just as explorers navigate water bodies, data engineers navigate data lakes, extracting valuable insights when the time is right. These lakes empower organizations to dive into the depths of data, uncovering hidden gems of knowledge.

Schema Design

Blueprints are essential for constructing any complex structure, be it a building or a data system. In data engineering, schema design is the blueprint that defines how data is structured, organized, and related. Data engineers design schemas that determine the structure of databases and how data elements are interconnected. Effective schema design ensures data is organized, accessible, and serves its intended purpose.

Let's look through the principles:

Data governance, data quality, reliability, scalability, security, ethics, and interoperability are quintessential in data engineering. These guiding lights illuminate our path as we navigate the complex terrain of modern data systems. Let's explore each principle in greater detail, understanding its essence and impact.

Data Governance

At the heart of effective data engineering lies data governance—a framework that ensures data is managed consistently and responsibly. Data governance orchestrates data across the organization. This principle establishes rules, standards, and procedures for data management, safeguarding its accuracy, integrity, and accessibility.

Data Quality

Quality in data isn't just a desirable trait; it's an imperative. Data quality ensures that the information fueling insights is reliable and accurate. Informed decision-making is based on high-quality data, which aids firms in their quest for success.

So, data engineers clean, validate, and enrich data to fulfill strict criteria, just as a sculptor removes imperfections from a work of art.

Reliability

Reliability in data engineering ensures that systems consistently produce accurate results, even in the face of challenges. Whether it's system failures or surges in demand, reliability stands firm. Through redundancy, fault tolerance, and disaster recovery strategies, data engineers guarantee data systems are unwavering and trustworthy.

Scalability

As organizations grow, so does the volume of data. Scalability ensures that data systems have the elasticity to accommodate this growth without compromising performance. Just as a building's foundation supports its rising structure, scalability empowers data systems to adapt to changing demands (Hurwitz *et al.*, 2013). Through horizontal scaling, cloud technologies, and distributed architectures, data engineers pave the way for sustainable growth.

Security

In the digital realm, security is paramount. It ensures data remains confidential and protected from breaches. Security mechanisms shield data from unauthorized access, malicious threats, and vulnerabilities. Encryption, access controls, and audit trails fortify the data fortress, preserving its sanctity.

Ethics

As data engineers, we are entrusted with an ethical responsibility. The ethical principle underpins our actions, urging us to handle data with integrity, respect privacy, and use data ethically. Data engineers embrace an ethical oath (like doctors' Hippocratic oath), promising to uphold the rights and dignity of data subjects.

Interoperability

In a world of diverse data sources and systems, interoperability bridges gaps and facilitates seamless data exchange. Interoperability ensures data speaks a common language. Through standardized formats, APIs, and integration tools, data engineers create an interconnected data ecosystem.

I'm struck by the realization that data engineering is a symphony composed of concepts and principles that harmonize to create robust, reliable, and innovative data-driven masterpieces. From data pipelines to schema design, these concepts and principles interweave to orchestrate the movement, transformation, and utilization of data. Data engineers blend concepts to create insights that resonate with businesses and drive innovation with accuracy, trustworthiness, and utility.

Data Collection Techniques and Best Practices

In data engineering, data collection serves as the cornerstone of insights and innovation. It's the process of systematically gathering and procuring information from diverse sources, with the ultimate aim of transforming raw data into actionable intelligence. This pivotal stage lays the foundation upon which decisions are made, strategies are devised, and solutions are crafted.

Data Collection Techniques

Surveys

By drawing from a bigger pool of respondents, surveys give us a comprehensive picture of views and trends.

Interviews

Contrarily, conducting interviews with a smaller, more narrowly focused group enables in-depth exploration.

Focus Groups

Focus groups present a structured platform for a small number of participants to discuss a particular topic, lending itself to interactive insights.

Observational Studies

Observational studies involve watching events unfold without direct interaction, making it a valuable approach to understanding natural behavior.

The essence of selecting the right technique lies in assessing factors such as the study's purpose, the intended audience, the available budget, and the constraints on time.

Best Practices

To ensure success in data collection, a set of best practices serves as a guiding compass.

Firstly, you should begin with a crystal-clear comprehension of your data requirements. This foundational step sets the tone for the entire process.

Next, select a data collection approach that best matches the goals of your project.

The third practice involves meticulous planning. A well-structured plan accounts for variables, resources, and the overall timeline.

Collecting data consistently and reliably forms another cornerstone. Consistency across different points of data collection is vital to maintain data integrity.

Once collected, data should be cleaned and prepared meticulously for analysis. This step is pivotal in ensuring the accuracy of insights derived.

Finally, don't overlook the significance of documenting your data collection process. A well-documented process can aid in replication, verification, and even correction, if necessary.

As you start data collection, there are some mistakes to avoid. First, resist the urge to gather an excessive amount of data. Overwhelming yourself with a deluge of information can obscure the real insights you're seeking. Moreover, data collection should always be purpose-driven. Collecting data that isn't relevant to your project can result in a sea of noise, drowning out meaningful patterns.

Always collect data consistently (method-wise). Inconsistencies can introduce bias and undermine the reliability of your findings. The essential step of cleaning and preparing data should never be compromised. Ignoring this stage can lead to skewed conclusions and faulty insights.

Lastly, document, document, document. The transparency, reproducibility, and overall credibility of your work might be compromised by not recording the data collection procedure.

Don't forget that each data collection technique is unique on its own. Surveys tap into the power of numbers, interviews delve into personal narratives, focus groups foster interactive discussions, observational studies uncover unfiltered behaviors, and experiments manipulate variables to reveal causal relationships. The scope, target audience, and aims of your project will all influence which technique is most appropriate.

Maintaining knowledge of these methods and abiding by best practices will help to ensure successful, dependable, and useful data collecting in the ever-changing field of data engineering.

Data Modelling and Schema Design

In the realm of databases, crafting a blueprint that organizes and structures data is akin to laying the foundation for a grand architectural masterpiece. This blueprint is known as a data model schema. In simpler terms, a data model schema spells out the arrangement of the database, defining the entities (or tables), the attributes (columns), and the intricate relationships that bind them together (Simsion & Witt, 2004). With this blueprint in hand, you're armed with a guide to not only construct the database but also ensure that data is stored in a manner that's coherent and logical.

Picture the schema as the architectural blueprint for your digital abode. It does more than simply provide a framework; it guides the entire construction process. In the realm of data, the schema's role is pivotal in maintaining the integrity of information. By establishing a consistent and systematic structure, it upholds the essence of data consistency and order. This orchestration extends beyond storage—it's a means to elevate the efficiency and performance of the database itself. Through the schema, redundancy is minimized, allowing for optimized storage and quicker access.

A schema ensures that data isn't just scattered randomly, but is organized in a way that is meaningful and functional. And a database schema is built with tables, columns, and relationships.

In the world of data, schemas are of paramount importance. They operate as the guardians of consistency and organization within the database. Beyond mere arrangement, they play a pivotal role in making data query-friendly, simplifying analysis, and fostering ease of access. The ripple effects extend further, impacting the performance of the entire database. You can create data that is both insightful and efficient by following a well-structured schema.

In the realm of data modeling, three distinct types of schemas reign supreme: logical, physical, and conceptual, these three types of schemas form the triad that shapes the database's life cycle.

Logical Schema

Imagine the logical schema as the master storyteller behind your data universe. It's the conceptual blueprint that maps out the intricate relationships between the various components of your database. This abstract construct goes beyond physical storage considerations and delves into the essence of how data elements interact.

At its core, the logical schema defines the structure of the data model in a way that's independent of any specific database management system (DBMS). Think of it as the map that guides you through the journey of data relationships, encapsulating entities (tables), their attributes (columns), and the connecting threads that link them. By doing so, the logical schema provides a panoramic picture of the data's interconnection, setting the framework for understanding the data's context and behavior.

Physical Schema

Now, let's transition from the abstract to the tangible with the physical schema. This is where the blueprint takes form in the physical world, determining how data is actually stored and accessed within a specific database management system. While the logical schema focuses on relationships and structures, the physical schema delves into the nitty-gritty of storage mechanisms, indexing, and performance optimization.

Picture the physical schema as the architect who brings the blueprint to life. It's concerned with the practical aspects of data storage — where it resides, how it's indexed for quick retrieval, and how it's organized on disk. This layer of the schema design involves decisions about file organization, table structures, indexing strategies, and other technical details that directly influence the database's performance.

Conceptual Schema

This level of schema design provides the big-picture perspective, aligning the database's purpose and objectives with the broader organizational goals. If the logical schema is the intricate design of a building, and the physical schema is its construction, then the conceptual schema is the overarching vision that guides both.

The conceptual schema is the realm of high-level abstraction, where you outline the database's scope, its role within the organization, and its alignment with business requirements. It connects technical complexity to decision-making strategies. I like to think of it as the database's mission statement that explains its existence, role, and use.

Data modeling, which breathes life into these schema concepts, is a craft that involves creating a logical representation of data. This intricate process defines the interplay of data's various facets, from relationships between entities to constraints that safeguard its integrity. On the other hand, schema design is the tangible act of translating this logical representation into a physical realm. It encompasses the specifics of data storage, indexing mechanisms, and constraints that shape the actual database structure.

The synergy between data modeling and schema design emerges as a crucial cornerstone for the database's lifecycle. Together, they ensure that data is housed in a manner that's not only consistent but also efficient. The dynamic duo paves the way for seamless querying, insightful analysis, and streamlined management. As you navigate the landscape of data engineering, remember that data modeling and schema design are your faithful companions, diligently working behind the scenes to fortify the foundations of your data-driven endeavors.

Data Validation and Cleaning

Ensuring the accuracy, completeness, and consistency of data is akin to preparing the canvas for a masterpiece. This is where data validation and cleansing step in, playing a pivotal role in preparing data for the journey through the analytics process. Think of it as the meticulous process of ensuring that your data is primed and polished before it's transformed into insights.

Data validation and cleansing are responsible for scrutinizing your data to ensure it meets the gold standard. It's the art of spotting errors, anomalies, and inconsistencies that may have sneaked into your dataset (Bienkwoski *et al.,* 2012).

The primary task of data validation involves scouring your dataset for potential pitfalls – missing values, invalid entries, and the elusive duplicate values that can muddy your analysis waters. Validation is all about detecting the issues that might compromise the integrity of your data. The steps involved in data validation include:

Step 1: Ensuring Accuracy

Imagine data validation as the diligent detective, meticulously searching for discrepancies and inconsistencies within your dataset. Firstly, you need to scan the data for missing values, outliers, and invalid entries that might throw off your analysis. This step is about ensuring that the data accurately represents the real-world scenario it aims to capture.

Step 2: Handling Missing Data

Once the detective work reveals gaps in your dataset, it's time to address the missing pieces. This step involves strategic decisions on how to deal with missing data points. Depending on the nature of the analysis, you might choose to ignore, replace, or estimate missing values based on context and available information. After this, your data is ready for analysis.

Step 3: Tackling Duplicate Data

Data validation involves identifying and handling these duplicates, as they can rubbish your analysis results. The process includes pinpointing duplicate records and deciding whether to remove them entirely or consolidate them into a single entry. This step helps to maintain the integrity of your dataset.

Once data validation has sounded the alert, it's time for data cleansing to take the stage. This is where errors are either corrected or ousted from the dataset. Data cleansing carefully chisels away inaccuracies to reveal the true essence of your data (Komatineni *et al.,* 2012). This step involves techniques that range from replacing erroneous entries to altogether removing problematic data points.

In data analysis, a single error can compromise your results. This is where data cleaning assumes center stage. It's the process of purging your data of inconsistencies and errors. By sifting through your dataset, data cleaning ensures that your analysis is built on a sturdy foundation.

You won't always use a particular technique when cleaning your data, the technique you employ depends on the nature of the data. Imagine you're restoring an antique painting – you'd use different methods for cleaning, repairing, and preserving. Similarly, data cleaning employs various strategies, such as error identification and correction, ridding your dataset of duplicate records, filling in the blanks where data is missing, formatting data uniformly, and standardizing data for consistency (Chapman, 2005).

Step 1: Correcting Errors

As data validation clears the path, data cleansing takes center stage. This step focuses on error correction. Just as a restorer mends a damaged artwork, you'll address inaccurate data entries. This might involve manually rectifying errors or applying algorithms to automatically correct entries that deviate from expected norms.

Step 2: Removing Outliers

Outliers, like unexpected guests at a party, can disrupt the harmony of your analysis. Data cleansing involves identifying and deciding how to handle these outliers. But keep in mind that you might not have to remove these outliers if they provide valuable insights into your work.

Step 3: Standardizing Formats

Imagine your dataset as a collection of puzzle pieces – each one must fit seamlessly to create the bigger picture. Data cleansing includes standardizing formats, ensuring that data is uniformly presented across the dataset. This might involve converting units, normalizing date formats, and aligning text capitalization.

Step 4: Ensuring Consistency

Consistency is the cornerstone of a robust dataset. Data cleansing involves harmonizing data to ensure that entries match predefined standards. This might entail aligning naming conventions, categorizations, and labels, creating a cohesive dataset that's a pleasure to work with.

Step 5: Final Review and Quality Assurance

Just before the curtain closes on the data cleaning process, a final review is in order. Think of it as the director's last glance before the opening night. This step involves scrutinizing the dataset to ensure that all errors have been corrected, inconsistencies resolved, and the data is primed for analysis.

In data analysis, your data cleaning technique will depend on the nature of your data set and the expected result. Just as a musician selects the right instrument for a particular melody, you'll choose your data-cleaning techniques with precision.

Data validation and cleaning are the gatekeepers, the artisans, and the curators of your data's journey to insight. By meticulously validating and cleansing your data, you're ensuring the integrity, accuracy, and reliability of your analysis. Remember, just as a clean canvas is the foundation of a masterpiece, data validation and cleaning are the bedrock of meaningful insights.

Data Integration and Transformation Strategies

Weaving the threads of information from different sources into a cohesive narrative is like crafting a mosaic masterpiece. This is where data integration and transformation strategies emerge as the architects of coherence, orchestrating the symphony of data for meaningful insights.

Data Integration Strategies

Data integration strategies are the roadmap to fuse varied data sources into a unified whole. Three key strategies stand out:

Extract, Transform, Load (ETL): ETL extracts data from multiple sources, transforms it into a consistent format, and then loads it into a target database. It's the time-tested approach that's akin to carefully curating ingredients before a grand feast.

Extract, Load, Transform (ELT): A newer approach gaining prominence, ELT extracts data, places it in a staging database, and then transforms it. It's like arranging puzzle pieces before revealing the final picture, offering flexibility and scalability.

In-memory Data Integration: Imagine storing your most prized possessions within arm's reach, rather than in a distant vault – that's the essence of in-memory data integration. This approach holds data in memory, boosting the swiftness of integration tasks.

Data Integration Challenges

Data Silos: These are like islands in a vast ocean, where data remains disconnected. The challenge is to bridge these silos to enable seamless data flow for analysis.

Data Quality: Think of your data as the raw material for your masterpiece. Poor data quality, laden with inaccuracies and inconsistencies, can lead to skewed analysis and misguided decisions.

Data Security: Data security shields your information from unauthorized access, ensuring its integrity and confidentiality.

Data Transformation Techniques

Imagine you're a sculptor molding raw clay into intricate forms – that's data transformation at work. This process shapes data to reveal hidden patterns and insights. It encompasses:

Data Cleaning: This is the meticulous process of removing errors and inconsistencies, ensuring your data shines like polished marble.

Data Integration: this combines diverse data sources into a coherent dataset.

Data Aggregation: Think of this as condensing a lengthy novel into a succinct synopsis – data aggregation summarizes complex information into manageable chunks.

Data Mining: Delve into the realm of data mining, where you're the explorer uncovering hidden gems within your data, revealing trends that were once obscured.

Data Transformation Challenges

Yet, as with any creative endeavor, challenges are part of the process. Data transformation faces challenges such as:

Data Volume: The deluge of data is growing exponentially, demanding efficient handling and transformation.

Data Complexity: Data transformation grapples with intricate data structures and relationships.

Data Velocity: Data arrives like a swift river, ever-flowing and evolving. Data transformation techniques must adapt to process this swiftly changing stream.

Choosing the Right Tools

Selecting the right tools for data transformation is about aligning capabilities with needs. The tools are:

Commercial Tools: These are like premium paints, offering advanced features and capabilities, though at a cost.

Open Source Tools: They're often free or budget-friendly, although with varying degrees of functionality.

Custom Tools: Just as an artist tailors their tools to their unique style, custom tools are designed to meet specific organizational needs.

Navigating the Selection Challenge:

However, choosing data transformation tools involves weighing factors such as:

Data Size and Complexity: The tool must be equipped to handle the sheer volume, intricacy, and pace of your data transformation needs.

Required Features and Functionality: Just as different artworks demand different tools, your specific transformation needs will dictate the required features.

Budget Alignment: The investment in tools should seamlessly align with your organization's financial scope.

In data integration and transformation, each strategy, technique, and tool assumes a vital role in sculpting raw data into invaluable insights. It's a journey that requires expertise, creativity, and a keen eye for detail, where the canvas of data becomes a masterpiece of knowledge.

Introduction to Data Warehousing and Data Lakes

Just take a moment to imagine data as a vast ocean, teeming with information waiting to be harnessed. In this digital expanse, data warehousing, and data lakes emerge as the anchor points where organizations store their treasures for future exploration.

Data Warehousing

Think of a data warehouse as a meticulously organized library, where books are systematically categorized for easy access. A data warehouse serves as a repository for historical data, meticulously cleaned, and structured for analytical purposes. This curated pool of information becomes the cornerstone for informed decision-making.

Data Lakes

Unlike a data warehouse, a data lake embraces the raw, unfiltered nature of data. It's a reservoir where organizations store all types of data, regardless of structure, format, or source. This open-minded approach allows for flexibility, nurturing a playground for innovation and exploration.

Key Distinctions

Storage and Structure:

Data Warehouse: Structured data finds its home here, with a well-defined schema. It's optimized for efficient querying and reporting, ideal for generating insights.

Data Lake: Both structured and unstructured data coexist harmoniously, reflecting the real-world messiness of information. It's a space that encourages experimentation and exploration, ideal for machine learning and uncovering hidden patterns.

Purpose and Flexibility:

Data Warehouse: It excels at providing structured, refined insights. It's your go-to for reporting, business intelligence, and structured analysis.

Data Lake: It enables innovative endeavors like machine learning, deep dives into unstructured data, and experimental analysis. While it offers flexibility, it might require more effort in management and analysis due to its unstructured nature.

Challenges

Data Warehouse: The structured approach assures accuracy and efficiency but can lead to rigidity in accommodating evolving data types.

Data Lake: The openness comes with the challenge of managing diverse data sources and maintaining data quality amidst the influx of raw information.

In the end, the choice between data warehousing and data lakes depends on your purpose.

Takeaway

- Data engineering principles form the bedrock upon which data systems are built and insights are uncovered.
- Establishing a consistent and systematic structure upholds the essence of data consistency and order.
- Efficient data collection, cleaning, validation, transformation, and integration are crucial for sculpting raw data into invaluable insights.

3

AI-POWERED DATA STORAGE AND MANAGEMENT

Evolution of Data Storage Technologies

Most of us can't imagine how life was before technology, so imagining a time before digital domains, where data was confined to physical forms is quite a stretch. But the past 90 years have witnessed the continuous evolution of data storage. We've traversed a remarkable journey from magnetic drums and tapes to hard disk drives, and further to the era of mixed media and lightning-fast flash storage. Finally, the horizon expanded to embrace the ethereal realm of cloud storage, a virtual haven for our data treasures.

Picture yourself in the early '90s, when the dawn of a revolutionary technology was marked by the introduction of the first commercial SSD. This innovation, heralded by SanDisk in 1991, boasted a modest storage capacity of 20 megabytes.

The evolution of data storage wasn't a mere coincidence; it was propelled by powerful forces. We started generating larger amounts of data and as expected, needed faster access to information. Simultaneously, there was an aspiration to drive down costs while optimizing storage capabilities. These factors converged to shape the trajectory of data storage's evolution.

Travel back even further, to a time when punched cards controlled automated textile looms in the 1800s. The roots of data storage, buried in the past, began with these primitive devices. The 1930s marked the advent of magnetic tape, a more efficient data storage method that is still relevant today, albeit overshadowed by the rise of hard disk drives.

Fast forward to the 1950s, the creation of hard disk drives was witnessed, and it introduced the arrival of storage powerhouses that continue to dominate today. Hard disk drives presented a remarkable leap in storage capacity and access speed, becoming the workhorses of data storage. They symbolize a remarkable intersection of technology and imagination, driving us forward.

I'm struck by the stark contrast between the first primitive storage devices and today's sophisticated marvels. The path of evolution has been filled with trials, triumphs, and tireless innovation, transforming how we preserve and harness data.

In the world we now inhabit, there isn't a singular form of data storage. Diversity reigns, and an array of storage devices have emerged, each with its unique advantages and challenges. This rich tapestry encompasses storage mediums that have evolved to cater to the ever-growing demands of data management.

The journey from punch cards to cloud storage showcases the power of human ingenuity, shaping the way we store, manage, and access information.

Introduction to Cloud Storage and Distributed Systems

Distributed computing breaks down data into manageable fragments. It's like assembling a gigantic jigsaw puzzle with friends, each tackling their piece independently. This process involves multiple computers working together, each solving its part of the puzzle. This teamwork not only accelerates the solution but also fosters efficiency and resilience in data processing.

Cloud Computing

Cloud computing is a place where data roams freely, where resources like servers, storage, and applications find their celestial abode on remote servers. These resources are accessed over the internet, erasing the boundaries of physical location. The cloud serves as a shared arena for computing resources, effortlessly accommodating various users and their data needs (Rueden *et al.,* 2017).

Cloud Storage

Imagine a network of interconnected servers, orchestrating a symphony of data storage. Cloud storage systems embrace the spirit of distributed systems, where data finds refuge on multiple servers, not confined to a single physical space. These systems are tailored to house vast volumes of data, from captivating images to captivating documents. This collective storage solution ensures data safety, availability, and accessibility, even amidst the vast expanse of the digital universe.

Differentiating Cloud Storage and Distributed Systems

Cloud storage focuses on housing data in remote locations, while distributed systems involve multiple computers working collaboratively to process and solve complex problems.

The Offerings of Cloud Storage Providers

Cloud storage providers are like vendors, each showcasing a distinct array of services. They specialize in delivering different types of storage, catering to diverse data needs. They are a haven for unstructured data; file storage, where files are organized and accessed with ease; and block storage, like digital building blocks forming the foundation of data structures.

Cloud storage is like a canvas where data finds its place among myriad servers. Imagine being able to retrieve your cherished data from any point, knowing that it's safeguarded and replicated across this intricate digital landscape (McEwen & Cassimally, 2013).

Reflecting on cloud storage and distributed systems, I'm reminded of how technology has granted us the power to transcend boundaries. We can now access and store data effortlessly, connecting the dots between our needs and the boundless capabilities of digital networks.

AI-Powered Data Cataloging and Metadata Management

AI-powered data cataloging and metadata management - a realm where artificial intelligence and automation unite to unlock the potential of data. In this realm, every piece of data is a storehouse of insights waiting to be discovered.

AI-Powered Data Cataloging

Have you ever wondered how data catalogs transform raw information into valuable assets? An AI-powered data catalog does just that, utilizing artificial intelligence and automation to gather, process, manage, and analyze metadata on a grand scale. It's like having an army of data elves, tirelessly organizing and documenting data's journey, ensuring it's accessible, traceable, and reliable.

The AI-powered data catalog process begins with data collection, where AI algorithms tirelessly scan and capture metadata from diverse sources. As you delve deeper, you discover the art of data discovery, where AI becomes your guide, illuminating the path to the information you seek. This process culminates in data lineage, a revelation of data's ancestry, helping you understand its origins and transformations.

With AI-powered data cataloging, data discovery becomes effortless. Imagine the benefits—data discovery becomes a breeze, data governance strengthens its grasp, and data risk diminishes. It's like having a treasure map that not only leads you to valuable data but also safeguards its authenticity and security.

AI and ChatGPT: Revolutionizing Metadata Management

Imagine AI and ChatGPT joining forces, like a dynamic duo of knowledge and automation. These technologies are revolutionizing metadata management tasks—data discovery, documentation, and lineage. It's as if they've deciphered the cryptic language of metadata, making it accessible and comprehensible to all.

Metadata management takes on the role of guarding data quality and compliance (Talha *et al.,* 2019). Picture metadata as the unsung hero, providing context to data, turning it from a mere string to an invaluable asset. It's like reading the cover of a book before delving into its contents, ensuring you understand its essence and origin.

The Role of Metadata

Metadata is like data's storyteller, enriching every piece of information with its context, source, and transformations. As you navigate the labyrinth of information, metadata acts as your guide, helping you make sense of the data maze. From technical details to business relevance, metadata holds the key to unlocking data's true potential.

In AI-powered data cataloging and metadata management, you're not just dealing with strings of characters; you're shaping narratives that drive decisions and innovations. Through the orchestration of AI algorithms and the insights of metadata, you're paving the way for a data-driven future that's both accessible and enlightening.

Leveraging AI for Efficient Data Storage and Retrieval

In data engineering, AI can become your ally in transforming storage and retrieval processes into efficient and strategic endeavors, helping you optimize data handling.

Countless times, I have wished I can clone myself to manage data tasks. If you're like me, then I'm letting you know that AI can step in as your virtual assistant, wielding its powers to automate laborious tasks like data classification, tagging, and indexing. It's like having a diligent helper who takes care of the mundane, allowing you to focus on the visionary aspects of your work.

Elevating Efficiency in Storage and Retrieval

AI can help unravel hidden insights within your storage ecosystem. With its knack for pattern recognition and trend analysis, AI optimizes data storage and retrieval. It's as if AI knows the secret paths within the labyrinth of data, guiding you towards storing less and retrieving faster. Imagine a world where data doesn't just sit idle but contributes actively to your pursuits.

Data Deduplication with AI:

AI can help automate data deduplication, curbing the duplication menace. Think of AI as the vigilant guardian that keeps your data realm clutter-free, reducing storage demands and enhancing efficiency.

Proactive Resource Allocation

AI's predictive prowess can actually help predict your storage needs. By foreseeing future demand, AI dynamically allocates resources to optimize storage performance. It's like having a storage system that evolves with your needs, never falling short or overburdening itself.

NetApp

NetApp's AI solutions harness machine learning and deep learning to help with your successful storage. With AI's touch, tasks are automated, performance escalates, and storage resources align like clockwork. It helps improve efficiency across your data landscape.

AI and Storage Optimization

Whether it's automatically classifying data, orchestrating data placement, or predicting future storage needs, AI ensures harmony in your storage resources. It's like having a symphony of data optimization, with AI as the master of efficiency.

In the world of data engineering, AI is not just a buzzword; it's a transformational force that optimizes, automates, and empowers. It's like having a companion on your data journey—a companion that brings efficiency, foresight, and strategic advantage to your storage and retrieval processes.

Managing Big Data: Scalability and Performance Considerations

Navigating the vast seas of big data requires more than just storage capacity—it demands the right balance of scalability and performance. Let's dive into the heart of managing big data and explore the intricate dance between scalability and performance.

Scalability

Scalability is your solution for large data amounts. It's about ensuring that your system can handle larger crowds (read: workloads) without sacrificing the smooth flow (read: performance). When we talk about big data, scalability means equipping your processing system to gracefully handle the increasing volumes, velocities, and varieties of data.

Performance

Performance is the capability to complete tasks swiftly and efficiently. The solution to the performance of your large amount of data is your sprinter, ensuring that data is processed within an acceptable time frame. It's not just about speed, but also about maintaining agility, so tasks are accomplished seamlessly.

When crafting a big data solution, performance and scalability are the architects that shape the blueprint. Performance ensures your data is processed as fast as possible, while scalability guarantees that the process is not affected by the 3Vs. It's like creating a car that accelerates swiftly and navigates seamlessly through any road conditions.

Enhancing your big data's scalability and performance is a lot of work. Design considerations play a crucial role in this process. Opting for the right hardware and software is like choosing the perfect canvas and brushes. Designing for parallel processing ensures that multiple parts of your solution work in harmony, much like different elements in a painting. Techniques like data compression act as the finishing touches, refining your masterpiece.

When scaling, using a distributed computing framework spreads the workload like sunlight, ensuring every corner thrives. Embracing NoSQL databases is like inputting a variety of data that coexist in harmony. And leveraging cloud computing is like providing a controlled environment that allows for the addition of more data while saving resources.

A successful big data solution hinges on the perfect interplay of scalability and performance. They are not just technical aspects but the heartbeats of a thriving data ecosystem.

Data Lifecycle Management and Archiving Strategies

Let's navigate data lifecycle management and archiving strategies—a journey to ensure that data remains protected, compliant, and accessible throughout its lifespan. Data Lifecycle Management (DLM) oversees data from creation to deletion. This process includes data classification, retention, storage, and disposal, DLM ensures that data is accounted for, well-maintained, and ready when needed.

DLM plans each phase of data—creation, classification, storage, and eventual disposal, ensuring that data is stored efficiently, complies with regulations, and remains readily accessible. With DLM, you're empowered to manage your data's journey, safeguarding it from storms and ensuring it reaches its destination safely.

Archiving

Data archiving preserves data's legacy, moving it from active storage to a less accessible but secure location. This strategy frees up space on active storage while preserving data for long-term retention. Archiving can happen both on-premises and in the cloud, promoting preservation and accessibility.

Various Approaches to Archiving

Tape libraries are cost-effective and store vast amounts of data, yet accessing them can be slow, much like carefully retrieving a rare manuscript. Alternatively, the cloud offers a contemporary twist, offering scalability, flexibility, and ease. Yet, cloud-based archiving may come with higher costs.

Crafting a Data Archiving Strategy

1. Identify Data for Archiving

Identify data that needs archiving based on relevance, compliance, and long-term retention.

2. Set Retention Periods

Determine how long each type of data should be archived. Comply with regulations and business needs.

3. Choose the Right Solution

Opt for the right archiving solution. Whether tape libraries or the cloud, consider scalability, cost, and accessibility.

4. Implement with Precision

Implement the chosen strategy, ensuring seamless integration with existing systems.

5. Monitor and Maintain

Consistently monitor and maintain your archiving solution. Regularly review data relevance, security, and compliance.

Data lifecycle management and archiving are not just tasks but guiding principles—a map to safeguarding data's integrity, accessibility, and historical significance.

Data Security and Privacy in AI-driven Environments

A world where AI systems collect, analyze, and utilize personal data, poses intricate questions about privacy protection. We find ourselves facing the rising challenges of AI-driven environments. These environments trigger debates and discussions, where policymakers must craft new laws and regulations to protect our privacy in this era of rapid AI growth.

AI systems grapple with vast amounts of personal data. They scour social media posts, financial transactions, and medical records—each piece potentially holding a glimpse into our lives. The sheer volume of data presents a monumental challenge. AI systems need guidance to distinguish between valuable insights and potential intrusions. AI systems can trace our steps and unveil our activities, with technology unraveling our daily routines. This power to infer sensitive information prompts us to ponder the boundaries between technological advancement and personal privacy.

Protecting Against Security Risks

As we journey through the seas of data engineering, let's shift our focus to safeguarding AI systems from security risks. These systems require vigilant protection against looming cyber threats. AI is especially a target for cyberattacks because of its method of data collection, storage, and processing.

AI-powered chatbots are like modern-day scribes and are capable of weaving fictional tales that blur reality. These chatbots can produce fake news articles and deceptive social media posts, casting doubt on what's true and false. Securing AI systems means also ensuring that the information they disseminate is accurate and reliable.

AI systems can unknowingly perpetuate biases present in the data they're trained on. Ensuring AI systems don't discriminate is a critical responsibility.

Embarking on this data engineering venture, we grapple with the intricate balance between data's importance and the privacy rights of individuals. Organizations must navigate these waters with precision. While it is important to collect the necessary data to train and develop AI systems, individual privacy must also be protected. Anonymization and pseudonymization emerge as shields against potential privacy violations.

To maintain privacy and security, we need to implement security measures like encryption methods to defend against cyber attacks, and shield sensitive data, and also prioritize transparency and accountability (Wylde *et al.*, 2022). Organizations as well should be transparent with their AI systems, disclosing how data is used. This will help users navigate the systems more confidently.

We can also foster awareness about AI's potential and pitfalls, educating people about privacy risks so they can make informed decisions.

As we traverse the complexities of data security and privacy in AI-driven environments, envision a partnership—between you, me, and the evolving world of technology. This partnership calls for vigilant guardianship, where innovation and protection harmoniously coexist. In this landscape, let's embrace the role of stewards, navigating the currents of advancement while ensuring privacy and ethical standards remain our guiding stars.

Takeaway

- Innovation will always cater to man's growing needs.
- AI optimizes, automates, and empowers.
- When it comes to data storage, technology has granted us the power to transcend boundaries

PART II

ADVANCED TECHNIQUES IN DATA ENGINEERING

Moving away from the foundation of data engineering, which entails the somewhat stressful tasks of data collection and cleaning, we're now turning to the remaining parts of our job: the 'advanced techniques.' But even here, AI can still shoulder the heavy lifting, and with AI as your partner, you will learn to process data and deal with errors and anomalies like a pro.

After processing your data, we'll go into how to turn data into captivating visuals that other people can easily understand.

4

DATA PROCESSING AND ETL WITH AI

Understanding ETL Processes

ETL stands for Extract, Transform, and Load—a trilogy of tasks that ensures data flows seamlessly from source to destination. ETL amalgamates data from multiple sources, reshapes it, and then carries it to its final destination, often a data warehouse or another storage system.

The Three Phases of ETL

1. Extraction

This is where we gather data from its sources. ETL extracts data through various methods like database queries, file transfers, or even web scraping to collect digital treasures (Mayer & Cukier, 2013). This phase is all about obtaining raw data from its native habitats.

2. Transformation

This is where raw data transforms. It's cleaned, formatted, and manipulated to fit the requirements of the target system. Here, ETL engineers ensure that data is polished and perfected.

3. Loading

This is where the transformed data finds its new home, be it a data warehouse, a data mart, or even a cloud-based data lake.

The Complexity of ETL

As we traverse these data seas, it's essential to recognize the significance of ETL in modern business. ETL is the bridge between diverse data sources and the insights organizations seek, ensuring that data is ready for use, and a necessity for organizations that want to make data-based informed decisions (Phillips-Wren *et al.*, 2015).

We've looked at the concept of ETL, but what's vital to understand is the sheer diversity of data sources it can integrate. ETL can handle data from operational databases, CRM systems, marketing platforms, and more. It's the ultimate data polyglot, enabling organizations to merge data from different sources into a common format for analysis and business intelligence.

It's no secret that navigating these data waters can be complex and time-consuming. However, businesses recognize that this complexity is the price of admission to the world of informed decisions.

ETL processes, although intricate, are the backbone of modern data analytics. They ensure that the data collected from various sources can be transformed into insights that steer organizations toward brighter horizons.

Enhancing ETL Pipelines with AI and Machine Learning

As a data engineer responsible for orchestrating the movement of data within an organization, ETL is your trusty vessel, used to Extract data from various sources, Transform it into a usable format, and Load it into a data warehouse. But imagine AI and ML are also essential tools that help automate and optimize every step of this process. I already mentioned in Part 1 how AI makes things a lot easier, you should know, however, that combining AI with machine learning in your data engineering process makes the process smooth like butter.

Machine Learning is an AI subset that improves machine performance over time by teaching them to learn from data (Nafea, 2018). These machines, guided by algorithms, can make predictions, identify patterns, and even make decisions without explicit programming.

Machine learning can be a potent ally. It's like having a team of tireless assistants. With ML, you can automate tasks that were once manual drudgery, such as data cleaning, feature extraction, and model training. This liberation allows data engineers to focus on the creative and innovative aspects of designing and implementing new data pipelines.

To truly appreciate the transformative power of AI and ML in ETL, let's examine specific applications:

1. Data Cleaning

ML can swiftly identify and remove errors and anomalies from your data. Clean data ensures the accuracy of your machine-learning models.

2. Feature Extraction

ML algorithms can automatically extract valuable features from your data. This feature-rich data fuels your models' performance, saving you time and effort.

3. Model Training

ML models can be trained to predict missing data values or even identify fraudulent transactions.

The Essence of ETL in Machine Learning

Now, let's shift our focus to ETL's pivotal role in the realm of machine learning. ETL is the one that ensures your machine learning models receive high-quality, clean, and consistent data.

Here are specific ways ETL works its magic to elevate machine learning models:

1. Data Cleaning

ETL identifies and eliminates data errors and anomalies, ensuring your machine learning models work with clean, reliable data. It's the foundation for model accuracy.

2. Feature Engineering

ETL creates new features from existing data, enhancing your models' performance, and aiding machine learning insights.

3. Data Preparation

ETL prepares data for machine learning by normalizing it and dividing it into training and test sets. This step ensures your models are trained on the best-quality data, setting them up for success.

It is evident that AI, ML, and ETL have charted a new course for data pipelines. They've liberated data engineers, empowered data cleansing, supercharged feature extraction, and paved the way for more accurate machine learning models.

ETL is no longer just a process; it's an evolving practice, shaping the future of data engineering. So, as you embark on your data adventures, remember that with AI, ML, and ETL by your side, the possibilities are limitless (Bergh *et al.*, 2019).

Streamlining Data Processing and Workflow Automation

As a data engineer navigating the intricate waters of data integration, it is not uncommon to find yourself performing repetitive tasks like data cleansing, validation, and transformation. This is where workflow automation comes to your rescue. It's like having a crew of diligent assistants automating these tasks, leaving you with more time to strategize and innovate.

Workflow automation is a game-changer in data integration. It not only enhances efficiency but also acts as a guardian against human errors that can sneak into data processes. Additionally, it offers the flexibility to adapt to changing data sources and requirements seamlessly.

Benefits of Workflow Automation

1. Increased Efficiency

Workflow automation dramatically reduces the time and effort required to integrate data. It's like turbocharging your data pipeline, allowing it to process information swiftly and accurately.

2. Improved Accuracy

With automation, the risk of human error diminishes significantly. Say goodbye to manual slip-ups, as automated workflows ensure precision in data integration.

3. Enhanced Flexibility

Data landscapes evolve, and so should your processes. Workflow automation provides the agility needed to accommodate changes in data sources and requirements. It's as adaptable as a ship's sails, adjusting to the wind's direction.

Navigating Business Data

Now, let's move on to streamlining your business data. Your data is the treasure chest of your organization, and efficient workflows are the keys to unlocking its full potential. To achieve this, automation becomes your closest ally:

1. Data Integration Platforms

Use specialized platforms to automate the movement of data between different systems, some of these platforms include Fivetran, Informatica, Dell Boomi, and Cleo Integration Cloud.

Practical Steps

- Choose Your Platform: There are many options like Apache Nifi, Talend, and Apache Camel. Select one based on your specific needs.
- Connect Data Sources: Configure your platform to connect to your data sources. This usually involves providing connection details like database credentials or API keys.

- Design Data Flows: Create data pipelines that define how data moves from source to destination. Specify transformations and actions along the way.
- Schedule Automation: Set up schedules to automate data transfers, maybe fetching data from a database by 2 am every day.

2. Workflow Management Tools

Employ these tools to automate various steps in your business processes, guiding you through the maze of data workflows. An example is Apache Airflow, an efficient tool for automating your data pipeline, it also runs multiple tasks such as looping through the source directory, running ETLs, posting to Slack, sending mails, etc on a single host. Another example is Centerprise

Practical Steps

- Choose Your Tool: Options include Apache Airflow, Microsoft Power Automate, or UiPath. Pick one that suits your workflow needs.
- Define Your Workflow: Outline the series of tasks or processes you want to automate. Start simple; you can always expand later.
- Design Workflow Steps: Create a visual representation of your workflow. This might involve creating flowcharts or using the tool's interface.
- Set Triggers: Define what triggers your workflow. It could be a specific time, a file arriving in a folder, or an API call.
- Automate Actions: For each step in your workflow, specify what action needs to be taken. For instance, send an email, update a database, or generate a report.

3. Scripting

For the hands-on approach, scripting allows you to craft custom automation solutions or codes tailored to your specific needs.

Practical Steps

- Choose Your Language: Popular scripting languages include Python, JavaScript, and PowerShell. Choose the one you're comfortable with or interested in learning.
- Identify Tasks: Start with a specific task you want to automate. It could be file renaming, data manipulation, or report generation.
- Write Your Script: Use your chosen scripting language to write the code for your automation. Break complex tasks into smaller, manageable steps.
- Test Thoroughly: Before deploying your script, test it rigorously. Make sure it performs as expected and handles potential errors gracefully.
- Schedule Execution: Use tools like cron jobs (for Unix-based systems) or Task Scheduler (for Windows) to schedule when your script should run.

Simplifying Data Entry

Having to input data day in and day out manually can be a time-consuming and error-prone process. But even here, automation can help get rid of that.

1. Data Entry Software

Utilize specialized software to automate the process of entering data into computer systems. It's like having an efficient crew that handles this task swiftly, and eliminates the need for manual keystrokes, saving you time and reducing errors.

Practical Steps

- Select Your Software: Start by choosing the right tool for your needs. Options include tools like Robotic Process Automation (RPA) software, UIPath, or Automation Anywhere.
- Install and Configure: Install your chosen software and configure it according to your data entry requirements. This may include setting up user access and permissions.
- Record Data Entry Steps: Use the software's recording feature to capture the exact steps you take during a typical data entry task. This creates a script that can be replayed automatically.
- Customize Data Entry Rules: Define rules and validations for data entry. For instance, specify which fields are mandatory and what formats are acceptable.
- Schedule Automation: Set up schedules for your data entry tasks, and put a specific time for when they should run and how long.

2. Robotic Process Automation (RPA) Tools

RPA tools automate repetitive tasks, including data entry with precision and faster than human data entry operators.

Practical Steps

- Choose Your RPA Tool: There are many options available, including UiPath, Blue Prism, and Automation Anywhere. Select one that aligns with your business needs.

- Identify Data Entry Tasks: Begin by identifying the data entry tasks you want to automate. It could be invoice processing, order entries, or customer data updates.
- Design RPA Bots: Create RPA bots or scripts that mimic the steps a human would take to enter data. These bots can interact with applications just like human operators.
- Test and Debug: Thoroughly test your RPA bots on sample data to ensure they perform accurately. Debug any issues that arise.
- Deploy Bots: Once your bots are ready, deploy them to perform data entry tasks according to your defined schedules or triggers.

3. Cloud-Based Data Entry Services

These services are like hiring external experts to handle your data entry needs. They not only streamline the process but also securely manage your data.

Practical Steps

- Choose a Provider: Research and select a reputable cloud-based data entry service provider. Ensure they meet your security and compliance requirements.
- Data Sharing: Share the data you want to be entered with the service provider. This might involve uploading files to a secure cloud storage location.
- Define Entry Rules: Clearly specify the rules and standards for data entry. Provide templates or guidelines to ensure consistency.
- Regular Updates: Set expectations for regular data updates and reporting. Define how often you want the service provider to perform data entry tasks.

- Monitor Performance: Keep an eye on the quality and timeliness of data entry tasks. Most providers offer dashboards or reports for monitoring.

Don't forget that workflow automation is the compass that guides data engineers and organizations through the intricate seas of data integration. It's the key to efficient, accurate, and adaptable data processes (Dumas *et al.*, 2018).

Real-time Data Processing with AI-driven Technologies

First, let's understand what real-time data processing entails. Unlike batch processing, where data is collected and processed in periodic chunks, real-time data processing is like capturing the essence of data as it emerges, much like catching a wave at the perfect moment.

AI and Real-Time Data Processing

AI is like the lighthouse guiding us through the ever-changing tides of data. It enhances real-time data processing in various ways:

Identifying Patterns and Anomalies

AI can swiftly identify patterns and anomalies in data as it flows in real-time. This capability is invaluable in detecting fraud, preventing outages, and providing impeccable customer service.

Making Predictions

AI doesn't just observe; it also predicts. By analyzing real-time data, it can forecast demand, optimize inventory, and guide us in making informed decisions.

Automating Tasks

As you've learned already, AI takes over routine tasks. With AI automation, you can redirect your human resources toward strategic endeavors while mundane tasks are expertly managed.

Charting a Real-Time Data Strategy

AI is critical in developing and implementing a real-time data strategy. It automates tasks, detects trends and abnormalities, and makes predictions, allowing organizations to use their data to gain a competitive advantage.

Real-Life Applications of AI in Real-Time Data Processing

Now, let's explore some tangible scenarios where AI is shaping the landscape of real-time data processing:

Fraud Detection

AI is the vigilant guardian of transactions, analyzing data in real-time to identify suspicious patterns and prevent fraudulent activities.

Outage Prevention

Sensors and AI work hand in hand to monitor equipment performance in real-time, foreseeing potential problems before they disrupt operations.

Customer Service Excellence

AI provides real-time insights into customer behavior, helping businesses swiftly identify and resolve issues, elevating the customer experience.

AI Transforms Manufacturing

In the manufacturing sector, real-time data and AI are revolutionizing processes. They enable quicker decision-making, heightened efficiency, and cost reduction.

Product Quality Control

AI watches over production lines, identifying defects in products as they occur. This improves product quality and reduces waste.

Supply Chain Optimization

AI optimizes supply chains by analyzing data from suppliers and customers, reducing costs and enhancing efficiency.

Asset Management

AI keeps a watchful eye on assets, predicting potential problems and scheduling maintenance to prevent downtime and maximize uptime.

With AI by your side, you can harness the full potential of real-time data, making data engineering smoother, more efficient, and filled with insights that guide your organization toward success.

Stream Processing Frameworks

Instead of saving received data first, stream processing allows us to analyze it as it comes in (Friedman & Tzoumas, 2016). This real-time method is suitable for real-time analytics, fraud detection, and other applications that need high throughput and low latency.

Stream processing is ideal for applications that call for quick insights because it enables us to study data as it flows in real-time. Whether it's detecting fraudulent transactions or monitoring IoT devices, these frameworks are the compass guiding us through the tumultuous seas of data. In datasets, it's normal to experience a number of stream processing frameworks, each with its unique strengths and quirks. Some of these frameworks include Apache Spark, Apache Storm, Apache Flink, and Amazon Kinesis Streams. And selecting the best framework depends on your specific needs.

Considering Your Requirements

Data Volume and Velocity

How much data will you be handling, and how fast is it flowing? Certain frameworks excel in handling massive streams.

Latency Requirements

Are you on a tight schedule? Some frameworks guarantee low latency, ensuring data gets processed swiftly.

Preferred Programming Language

You should favor a framework compatible with your programming language of choice.

The Frameworks at a Glance

1. Apache Spark

Strengths: Apache Spark is known for its versatility. It can handle both batch and stream processing, making it an excellent choice for organizations that require a unified data processing platform. Its built-in libraries for machine learning and graph processing are like treasure chests for data scientists.

Weaknesses: While Spark is incredibly versatile, it might not be the fastest option for pure stream processing tasks, especially when dealing with high-velocity data streams.

2. Apache Storm

Strengths: Apache Storm is dependable, tolerant, and designed for low-latency environments, which makes it perfect for real-time stream processing.

Weaknesses: Storm's learning curve can be steep, and it may require more configuration compared to other frameworks. It's primarily a stream-processing tool and lacks some of Spark's batch-processing capabilities.

3. Apache Flink

Strengths: Apache Flink is all about speed. It offers low-latency processing with event time semantics, making it perfect for applications requiring precise timing. Its support for event-driven applications and event time processing sets it apart.

Weaknesses: While Flink excels in performance, it may not be as straightforward to set up and configure as Spark or Storm. Users often need a strong understanding of event time processing to unlock its full potential.

4. Amazon Kinesis Streams

Strengths: As part of the AWS ecosystem, Amazon Kinesis Streams provides seamless integration with various AWS services. It's like a cloud-powered vessel, enabling easy scaling and management. Its simplicity and scalability are its greatest assets.

Weaknesses: Being cloud-native, Kinesis Streams may come with additional costs, especially for high-velocity data streams. It's also tightly coupled with AWS, which may limit flexibility for organizations using other cloud providers.

Selecting the right framework

Choose Apache Spark if you need a versatile solution that can handle both batch and stream processing, and you want to leverage its rich ecosystem for machine learning and analytics.

Opt for Apache Storm if your primary focus is real-time stream processing with low latency, and you're willing to invest time in mastering its unique architecture.

You can go for Apache Flink if speed and precision are paramount, and you're comfortable diving into the intricacies of event time processing.

Navigate the Amazon Kinesis Streams if you're in the AWS ecosystem, require easy scaling, and prefer a managed, cloud-native solution.

The success of your journey depends on the framework you choose. Each has its strengths and weaknesses, so, whether you're charting a course for real-time analytics, fraud detection, or IoT monitoring, may your choice of framework help you achieve success.

Real-Time Predictive Analytics Using AI Models

Real-time predictive analytics offers an opportunity to analyze data as it unfolds, opening doors to immediate insights and actions. Real-time predictive analytics, simply put, involves using AI models to examine data as it happens. This vital tool allows you to see anomalies, predict patterns, and act quickly on new possibilities or dangers, which optimizes operations, improves customer experiences, and protects your company's interests.

AI models breathe life into this real-time predictive analysis process, allowing you to decipher data on the fly. The benefits are manifold; you can combat fraud in financial transactions, predict customer churn, and optimize your inventory—all in real time. It's like having a skilled lookout at the crow's nest, spotting opportunities and threats long before they reach your shores.

AI is like the engine that drives the ship of prediction. It automates the tedious tasks of data preparation, feature engineering, and model training. The result? More precise and reliable models, crafted with less effort. These models, help you make swift and informed decisions as you sail through uncharted waters. It automates the predictive analytics process, making it faster and more accessible, by helping you gain insights from your data quickly. And when speed is your ally, you can act swiftly to enhance your performance and seize new horizons.

Steps in Building Real-Time Predictive Analytics Frameworks

Building real-time predictive analytics frameworks involves a structured workflow. Here are the five essential steps:

1. Data Collection

Data Sources: Identify the sources of real-time data. This could be streaming data from IoT devices, social media feeds, or transaction records.

Data Ingestion: Set up processes to ingest data in real time. Tools like Apache Kafka or RabbitMQ can help with this.

2. Data Preprocessing

Cleaning: Handle missing data, outliers, and errors. In real-time, this often involves on-the-fly data cleansing.

Feature Engineering: Select relevant features and transform them as needed for analysis. In real-time, feature engineering should be efficient and adaptive.

3. Model Selection

Algorithm Choice: Select the appropriate classification or regression algorithm based on your problem. In real-time, consider algorithms optimized for low-latency predictions.

4. Model Training and Deployment

Training: Train your model using historical data. In real-time, this model can be incrementally updated with new data.

Deployment: Deploy your model in a real-time environment where it can make predictions as new data arrives.

5. Monitoring and Maintenance

Monitoring: Continuously monitor model performance. Set up alerts for when the model's predictions deviate from expectations.

Feedback Loop: Implement a feedback loop where model predictions inform decision-making, creating a closed-loop system that adapts to changing conditions.

These stages provide a systematic way to construct real-time predictive analytics frameworks, ensuring that your models remain exact and reliable in a dynamic, real-time environment.

Scalability and Fault Tolerance in Real-Time Data Processing

In the heart of real-time data processing, two formidable challenges stand tall: scalability and fault tolerance. As you might have guessed, both are tightly interwoven, affecting the efficiency and resilience of our data systems. The first challenge arises from the sheer magnitude of data - the volume, velocity, and variety are ever-increasing. It's like trying to handle an ever-expanding river of information.

The second challenge, fault tolerance, is equally crucial. Even the smallest inaccuracy can have catastrophic results in real-time data processing. Think about how the system would come to a complete stop if just one component failed.

Strategies For Solutions

1. Distributed Processing

Distributed processing involves spreading the workload across multiple nodes. This not only enhances scalability but also fortifies fault tolerance. If one ship encounters a storm, the others can carry on.

2. Replication

This is similar to making copies of important documents. Replication in data engineering refers to the process of making copies of data. In the event of a component failure, it can be quite helpful when done strategically. Other copies are available to fill in if one gets lost.

3. Checkpointing

Checkpointing in data systems entails periodically saving the system's state, so that if something goes wrong, you can restore a previously saved state.

The Relevance of Scalability and Fault Tolerance

While on the lookout for optimized real-time data processing, we need to understand why scalability and fault tolerance are important. As you venture deeper into this field, you'll discover that real-time data processing isn't stagnant but dynamic.

The Volume Challenge

As I mentioned in the part about the evolution of storage systems, the amount of data being generated in real-time keeps increasing, and without scalability, we'll struggle with data processing.

The Need for Low Latency

Real-time data processing requires managing massive amounts of data swiftly. Once you can't examine days quickly, you might end up using outdated information in your decision-making process.

The Reliability Imperative

Fault tolerance ensures that our data processing system remains steady even when faced with adversity.

As data engineers, our success in real-time data processing hinges on the twin pillars of scalability and fault tolerance. Armed with distributed processing, replication, and checkpointing, we're well-prepared to handle the increasing data volumes and the need for swift, resilient decision-making.

Performance Optimization and Error Handling Techniques

When it comes to Performance Optimization, we're talking about making your data pipelines sail smoothly and swiftly as optimizing your data engineering processes can significantly improve efficiency. Some of the techniques for performance optimization include:

Partitioning Data

This technique involves splitting large datasets into smaller, more manageable chunks, this way you'll process data in parallel, optimizing your available computing resources.

Parallel Processing

Parallel processing involves executing tasks concurrently. This technique harnesses the power of modern multi-core processors and distributed computing to get your data processed faster.

Caching Intermediate Results

Caching involves storing intermediate results during processing. If you require the same data again, you retrieve it rather than having to recalculate it. It's similar to having a handy map of your data.

Error Handling Mechanisms

Errors are the unpredictable waves and winds that can disrupt your progress. Effective error-handling mechanisms will however help you stay on course and save time.

Types of Errors in Data Engineering

1. Data Quality Errors

Missing Data: Sometimes, data is incomplete or entirely absent. Handling this error involves strategies like filling in missing data or setting default values.

Data Format Issues: Data might come in unexpected formats, causing processing errors. Here, data validation and transformation techniques come to your rescue.

2. Processing Errors

Runtime Errors: They include issues like division by zero, memory overflow, or system crashes. Proper error handling involves robust exception handling.

Logic Errors: Logic errors occur when your data processing steps are incorrect. Rigorous testing and debugging help identify and correct such issues.

3. Data Integration Errors

Data Mismatch: This is when data from different sources doesn't align. It's like trying to fit puzzle pieces from different sets together. Data integration errors often require data cleansing and transformation.

Duplicate Data: Duplicate data can mar your results. Detection and elimination of duplicates are vital to ensure data accuracy.

4. Network and Connectivity Errors

Data Transfer Failures: Network errors can hinder data flow. Handling these errors includes implementing data retry mechanisms and robust data transfer protocols.

System Outages: When your data processing system experiences downtime, it's like being stranded at sea. Implementing failover and backup systems is essential to ensure uninterrupted data processing.

Effective Error Handling Mechanisms

Now that we've identified the types of errors you might encounter in your data journey, let's discuss how to handle them effectively.

1. Logging

Logging involves taking records at every step of your data processing pipeline. When errors occur, these logs provide invaluable information for troubleshooting.

2. Alerting Systems

Alerting systems notify you of anomalies, and implementing alerting mechanisms that trigger when predefined error conditions are met ensures you're aware of issues in real time.

3. Graceful Recovery

Graceful recovery mechanisms allow your data processing to continue after the error occurs. This might involve retrying the failed operation, using backup data sources, or applying predefined error-handling strategies.

4. Continuous Monitoring

Continuous monitoring involves regularly checking the health of your data pipelines. Automated tools are advisable as they can detect issues before they escalate.

5. Documentation and Knowledge Sharing

Ensure your error-handling procedures are well-documented. This helps onboard new team members and ensures consistent error-handling practices.

If you're going to continue as a data engineer, you will often find yourself using tools and platforms tailored to your specific needs, choose the tools that suit your data projects best. You might employ indexing techniques, partitioning strategies, or parallel processing frameworks to optimize performance.

Similarly, for error handling, you'll implement mechanisms that align with your project's requirements. Robust logging, alerting systems, and automatic retries are just a few tools at your disposal.

Remember that data engineering is an evolving field. New techniques and tools are continuously emerging to help you sail through the data sea more efficiently and safely.

Takeaway

- ETL creates a bridge between diverse data sources and insights.
- Automation enhances efficiency and guides against human errors.
- Performance Optimization and Error Handling are vital to the data engineering process.

5

─────

AI-DRIVEN DATA TRANSFORMATION AND FEATURE ENGINEERING

Significance of Feature Engineering

I already mentioned feature engineering briefly in ETL processes, but here, we'll be doing an in-depth guide. Raw data is an ocean of information filled with valuable insights and information, and feature engineering is that tool that will help you assess the hidden information. Feature engineering transforms raw data into features that are not just relevant but also incredibly informative for machine learning algorithms. These features serve as the guiding stars for models, enabling them to navigate complex datasets. This transformative process can significantly impact a model's performance.

Techniques of Feature Engineering

Data cleaning: It involves tidying up the data, eliminating noise and outliers that can mislead your model.

Feature extraction: This involves creating new features from existing ones. This can reveal hidden patterns and relationships within your data.

Feature selection: Feature selection is about choosing the most important features for your model. This not only reduces complexity but also enhances the model's performance.

Feature transformation: Feature transformation involves changing the format of your features, such as normalizing or scaling them, so that your model can better understand and utilize them.

The Creative Art of Feature Engineering

It's not just a mechanical process but an art form that requires intuition and creativity. Feature engineering is a dance between data and algorithms, where you choreograph transformations to make your data speak the language of machines. It can be challenging to customize the feature engineering techniques to your needs, but don't forget that practice makes perfect.

Benefits of Feature Engineering

- It increases the precision of your machine-learning models, enabling you to make accurate predictions.
- It makes your models less complex and more efficient and easier to maintain.
- It enhances the interpretability of your models, helping you understand and trust their decisions.
- It fortifies your models against the turbulent seas of noisy and outlier-laden data.

So, don't forget, feature engineering is the key to unlocking the treasure trove of insights hidden within your data, and it will guide you to success in the ever-changing landscape of machine learning.

Automated Feature Extraction

Feature extraction is the second process in the feature engineering process that exposes needed information needed from large datasets after cleaning. Fortunately, automation has increased its effectiveness, accuracy, and adaptability.

Simply put, automated feature extraction is a specific method for automating the process of extracting meaningful information from data. It continuously sorts through data to find significant trends and characteristics. This streamlines the procedure and reduces the possibility of human error. You may speed up the creation of machine learning algorithms, improve the reproducibility of your findings, and spend less time and effort manually engineering features by automating feature extraction. It is comparable to having a full-time staff of data analysts at your disposal.

But there are challenges to face. The selection of features remains a critical decision. Too many features can lead to overfitting, while too few may result in a loss of critical information. So you need to strike a balance.

Moreover, optimizing feature extraction algorithms is like refining the tools of your trade. You need them to be efficient, accurate, and versatile. But you need to fully understand the data, the algorithms, and the problem at hand to find this balance.

Time Series Analysis and Feature Engineering

Before we dive into feature engineering, let's lay the groundwork by understanding what time series data is. Imagine you have data points collected over successive time intervals, such as daily stock prices, hourly weather data, or even monthly sales figures. Congratulations, you're dealing with time series data.

In the pursuit of knowledge within these data streams, we turn to feature engineering as our trusted guide. But, what exactly is feature engineering? In essence, it's the process of crafting informative attributes, or features, from raw data that can be readily consumed by machine learning models, for both supervised and unsupervised learning to simplify and speed up data transformations with accuracy. Now, let's explore how this concept applies specifically to time series data.

Three Paths to Feature Engineering

1. Statistical Feature Engineering

Here, we leverage statistical methods to extract essential features. Think of moving averages that smooth out erratic fluctuations, exponential smoothing that captures trends and seasonality, or Fourier transforms that unveil underlying periodic patterns. These techniques act as our compass, helping us navigate the complex terrain of temporal data.

2. Domain Knowledge Feature Engineering

This approach involves understanding the subject matter, identifying relevant patterns, and crafting features that encapsulate critical insights. For instance, in weather forecasting, recognizing seasonal patterns or spotting outliers can be the key to more accurate predictions.

3. Machine Learning Feature Engineering

This involves deploying algorithms like autoencoders or deep neural networks to automatically derive features from raw time series data. It's like having a data scientist at your side, tirelessly discovering hidden gems within your dataset.

The type of features we can find in large datasets include statistical features, which summarize data distributions, derivative features that measure changes over time, and even categorical features for encoding non-numeric information. The world of feature engineering is diverse and adaptable, offering a rich palette for crafting features tailored to your data's nuances.

But here's the real question: How do you choose the right features for your time series forecasting problem?

- Moving Averages: These smooth out noise and reveal underlying trends.
- Exponential Smoothing: Ideal for capturing seasonality and trends in your data.
- Fourier Transforms: Perfect for uncovering periodic patterns and frequencies.
- Wavelets: A versatile tool for both denoising and feature extraction.
- Lagged Features:These involve using past data points as features.
- Rolling Window Statistics: Calculating statistics over fixed time windows, unveils valuable insights.

With these techniques in your toolkit, you'll be equipped to tackle a wide array of time series data challenges, from stock market predictions to energy consumption forecasts.

Dimensionality Reduction Techniques for Large Datasets

In the ever-expanding universe of data engineering, one often encounters the challenge of dealing with vast datasets, rich in features and complexities. This is where dimensionality reduction steps in, offering a lifeline to navigate this data labyrinth. Imagine having a dataset teeming with features, but not all of them are equally informative. The concept of dimensionality reduction is similar to decluttering your workspace – it's about retaining essential information while discarding the noise.

Dimensionality reduction is the process of streamlining your dataset, aiming to preserve crucial information while reducing the number of features. Applications range widely, from improving machine learning model performance to streamlining data visualization. Different strategies are used to do this, each with certain advantages and uses.

Let's take a look at Principal Component Analysis (PCA), a linear technique that shines the spotlight on the most critical aspects of your data. It projects your data into a lower-dimensional space while preserving maximum variance. PCA excels in applications where capturing data variance is paramount.

Factor Analysis (FA) is a non-linear technique that delves deeper into the structure of your data. Instead of linear relationships, FA seeks underlying factors that explain data variation. Its strength lies in uncovering intricate patterns that might be missed by linear methods.

Linear Discriminant Analysis (LDA) takes center stage in situations where class separation is vital. LDA is a supervised technique that not only reduces dimensionality but also preserves the class separation between data points. It's your ally when you need to maintain critical information for classification tasks.

T-distributed stochastic neighbor embedding (t-SNE) and Multi-dimensional Scaling (MDS) are non-linear techniques tailored for visualization. They embed data points into lower-dimensional spaces while preserving inter-point distances. These techniques are like data maps, helping you map complex relationships with clarity.

Choosing the technique to use, as I've always emphasized, depends on the specifics of your application. You need to consider the number of features in your dataset, the type of data you're using, the level of precision you'd like, and the computing power you have available.

You must investigate, adapt, and experiment in order to make this decision. Your dataset is special, and the best dimensionality reduction method will depend on its complexity.

Dimensionality reduction empowers you to condense the complexity of your data, making it more manageable, interpretable, and conducive to analysis. It is not just about simplifying your data—it's about revealing its essence. It's about ensuring that you retain what truly matters while shedding the excess. With each dimension you reduce, you unveil new insights within your data.

Handling Missing Data Using AI-Driven Imputation Methods

As data engineers, we are always after complete, high-quality datasets. Although missing data is a typical problem that might impair the performance of machine learning models, it does occur from time to time.

Before we dive into AI-driven imputation, let's understand the basics. When confronted with missing data, you typically have two options: deletion or imputation. Deletion involves removing rows or columns with missing values, but it often results in data loss and reduced model accuracy. With imputation, however, we estimate and fill in those gaps of missing values.

Imputation is generally favored over deletion because it allows you to preserve more data, which as you know is a precious resource in the world of data engineering. There is a range of traditional imputation techniques available, and the three common methods include:

Mean Imputation: It involves filling the gaps with average values. You'll simply replace missing values with the mean average of observed values within a variable. Although it might not capture the true nature of the data, this method is simple and quick.

Median Imputation: If the mean is average, the median is the middle ground and it involves replacing missing values with the median of observed values. While it might reduce outliers, it can actually miss underlying patterns.

Multiple Imputation: This method involves generating several copies of the datasets, each with different imputed values. This technique helps reduce bias and provides a more accurate representation of uncertainty.

AI-Driven Imputation

AI-driven imputation methods represent a paradigm shift in handling missing data. Instead of relying on fixed statistical measures, these approaches leverage the power of machine learning algorithms to understand and impute missing values intelligently. The result? More accurate and data-driven imputations.

K-Nearest Neighbors Imputation: This method imputes missing values by seeking the k most similar rows with complete data and averaging their values. It's like asking your friends for their opinion and a collaborative approach to imputation.

Here's a step-by-step explanation of how K-NN imputation works:

1. Data Preparation: Start with a dataset that contains missing values for certain attributes or features. These missing values are the ones you want to impute.
2. Choosing K: Decide on the value of K, which represents the number of nearest neighbors to consider. To determine which K value works best for your dataset, you need to experiment with a few. A smaller K value will consider fewer neighbors, while a larger K value will consider more neighbors.
3. Distance Metric: Select an appropriate distance metric to measure the similarity between data points. Common distance metrics include Euclidean distance, Manhattan distance, or cosine similarity, depending on your dataset.
4. Identifying Neighbors: Measure the distance between every data point that lacks a value and every other data point in the dataset that is complete with the information required to answer the questioned attributes.
5. Selecting the Nearest Neighbors: Choose the K data points with the smallest distances to the point with missing values. These K data points are considered the nearest neighbors.
6. Imputation: Once you've identified the K nearest neighbors, you can impute the missing value by

aggregating or averaging the values of the corresponding attribute (feature) from these neighbors. Common aggregation methods include taking the mean, median, or weighted average of the attribute values from the neighbors. The choice of aggregation method depends on your specific problem and dataset.

7. Repeat for All Missing Values: Repeat steps d-f for all data points in your dataset that have missing values, imputing each missing value using its respective set of nearest neighbors.

8. Evaluation: After imputation, assess the quality of the imputed values, using evaluation metrics like Mean Absolute Error (MAE) or Root Mean Squared Error (RMSE) to measure how accurately the imputed values align with the actual values.

K-Nearest Neighbors imputation is effective when there's a reasonable assumption that similar data points share similar attribute values. It might not work effectively, though, if there are complicated interactions between the data points or if the dataset has a lot of dimensions. Careful consideration of the choice of K and the distance metric is crucial to the success of K-NN imputation.

Decision Tree Imputation: In this technique, a decision tree model is built to predict missing values. This machine-learning approach can be applied to both classification and regression applications. In the context of imputation, they are employed to predict missing values based on the relationships observed within the dataset.

Here's how Decision Tree imputation works:

1. Data Preparation: Begin with a dataset that contains missing values for certain attributes or features. These missing values are the ones you want to impute.
2. Selecting Attributes: Identify the attributes or features that are most relevant to the prediction of the missing values. These attributes will be used as input variables for the decision tree model.
3. Creating a Decision Tree: Build a decision tree model using the data points that have complete information for the attributes selected in the previous step. The decision tree will be trained to predict the missing values based on the patterns and relationships observed in the complete data.
4. Splitting Nodes: The decision tree recursively splits the data into subsets based on the values of the selected attributes. It chooses the attribute and the split point that best separates the data into groups with similar values for the missing attribute.
5. Leaf Node Values: Each leaf node of the decision tree corresponds to a specific combination of attribute values. The leaf nodes store the predicted values for the missing attribute based on the data points that fall into that node.
6. Imputation: For each data point with missing values, traverse the decision tree from the root node to a leaf node based on the attribute values available for that data point. The value stored in the leaf node where the traversal ends is used as the imputed value for the missing attribute.
7. Repeat for All Missing Values: Repeat 'f' for all data points in your dataset that have missing values, imputing each missing value using the corresponding leaf node of the decision tree.

8. Evaluation: After imputation, assess the quality of the imputed values, using evaluation metrics like Mean Absolute Error (MAE) or Root Mean Squared Error (RMSE) to measure how accurately the imputed values align with the actual values.

Decision Tree imputation can capture complex relationships between attributes and provide reasonably accurate imputed values. However, it has some limitations, such as overfitting, especially with deep trees, and the sensitivity to the choice of hyperparameters. Additionally, it may not perform well when there are no strong relationships between attributes or when the dataset is noisy. Careful tuning of the decision tree model's hyperparameters is crucial to obtaining the best results.

Random Forest Imputation: Like a forest of decision trees, this method constructs a random forest model to predict missing values. Random Forest imputation is a data imputation technique that leverages the power of ensemble learning using Random Forests to estimate missing values in a dataset. Random Forest is an ensemble machine-learning algorithm that consists of multiple decision trees. In the context of imputation, a Random Forest model is employed to predict missing values based on patterns and relationships observed in the dataset.

Here's how Random Forest imputation works:

1. Data Preparation: Begin with a dataset that contains missing values for certain attributes or features. These missing values are the ones you want to impute.
2. Selecting Attributes: Identify the attributes or features that are most relevant to the prediction of the missing values. These attributes will be used as input variables for the Random Forest model.

3. Creating a Random Forest: Build a Random Forest model using the data points that have complete information for the attributes selected in 'b'. The Random Forest is an ensemble of decision trees, each of which is trained to predict the missing values based on the patterns and relationships observed in the complete data.

4. Bootstrapped Samples: Random Forests use bootstrapped samples (random subsets of the data with replacement) to train individual decision trees. Each decision tree in the ensemble is trained on a different bootstrapped sample, introducing diversity into the models.

5. Random Feature Selection: At each node of each decision tree, a random subset of features is considered for splitting. This random feature selection further enhances the diversity among the trees.

6. Voting for Imputation: For each data point with missing values, all the decision trees in the Random Forest make individual predictions for the missing values based on the available attributes. The final imputed value is determined by aggregating the predictions, often through a majority vote for classification problems or an average for regression problems.

7. Imputation: Use the aggregated prediction as the imputed value for the missing attribute in the data point.

8. Repeat for All Missing Values: Repeat steps 'f' and 'g' for all data points in your dataset that have missing values, imputing each missing value using the majority-voted or averaged prediction from the ensemble of decision trees.

9. Evaluation: After imputation, assess the quality of imputed values using evaluation metrics like Mean Absolute Error (MAE) or Root Mean Squared Error (RMSE) to measure how accurately the imputed values align with the actual values.

Random Forest imputation offers several advantages, including robustness to overfitting, the ability to capture complex relationships between attributes, and the handling of both categorical and numerical features.

Deep Learning Imputation: Deep Learning imputation is an advanced technique for handling missing data using deep neural networks. It harnesses the power of deep learning models, which are artificial neural networks with multiple layers (deep architectures), to predict and impute missing values in a dataset. This method has grown in popularity because it can effectively capture intricate correlations and patterns in data, making it appropriate for datasets containing high-dimensional and organized information.

Here's how Deep Learning imputation works:

1. Data Preparation: Begin with a dataset containing missing values in some of its attributes or features. These missing values are the ones you aim to impute.
2. Data Preprocessing: Prepare the data by standardizing it, normalizing it, or encoding categorical variables if necessary. It's essential to ensure that the data is in a suitable format for training a deep learning model.
3. Architecture Selection: Choose an appropriate deep-learning architecture for imputation. Common choices include feedforward neural networks (FNN), convolutional neural networks (CNN), and recurrent

neural networks (RNN), among others, you can use either depending on the nature of the data and the problem at hand.

4. Model Training: Train the selected deep learning model using the dataset's complete observations (those without missing values). The model takes the available features as inputs and learns to predict the missing values based on patterns and relationships within the data. The training process involves multiple iterations (epochs) during which the model learns to minimize the error between its predictions and the actual values.

5. Validation: Use a portion of the data with complete observations (not used for training) to validate the model's performance. This step helps ensure that the model generalizes well to unseen data and provides reliable imputations.

6. Missing Value Prediction: Apply the trained deep learning model to predict the missing values in the dataset. The model takes the incomplete data points as input, and for each missing value, it generates a prediction. The predictions can be real-valued (regression) or class labels (classification), depending on the nature of the missing data.

7. Imputation: Replace the missing values in the dataset with the corresponding predictions generated by the deep learning model.

8. Post-Imputation Evaluation: After imputation, evaluate the quality of the imputed values, using Mean Absolute Error (MAE) or Root Mean Squared Error (RMSE), to assess how well the imputed values align with the actual values.

Deep Learning imputation offers several advantages, including its ability to capture intricate data patterns, handle high-dimensional data, and adapt to various data types (numerical, categorical, textual, etc.). However, it typically requires more data and computational resources than traditional methods and may be more susceptible to overfitting if not properly regularized. The number of layers, units per layer, and learning rate are only a few of the hyperparameters that deep learning models contain that may need to be tuned for optimum performance.

Feature Selection and Importance Estimation With AI Models

A significant step in this process of transforming raw data into actionable insights and one of the crucial steps in feature engineering is feature selection and importance estimation.

Feature selection involves picking a subset of features from a larger pool that is most pertinent to your predictive modeling task. The goal is to trim the excess and retain only the essentials. There are various techniques at your disposal for feature selection. Each method comes with its own strengths and weaknesses. Three prominent categories include:

Filter Methods: These rely on statistical properties of individual features, like their correlation with the target variable or variance, to decide their relevance.

Wrapper Methods: These methods build models using various feature subsets and select the one that results in the finest model performance.

Embedded Methods: Here, feature selection and modeling are intertwined, much like a well-composed symphony where each instrument plays a vital role.

Once you've pruned your feature set, the next step is understanding the importance of each remaining feature. Feature importance estimation involves assigning a score to each feature. This score signifies the relative importance of that feature in your predictive modeling endeavor.

Now, let's explore how AI models step into this realm to make your life easier.

Machine learning is strengthened by the use of AI models, which speeds up and improves the procedure.

AI-driven methods excel at identifying intricate patterns within your data. They go beyond simple statistical measures, learning the nuances of your dataset. This deep understanding allows them to make informed decisions regarding feature relevance.

AI-driven methodologies help your machine learning models perform better while also making them easier to understand.

Customizing Your Approach

Data engineering's versatility is one of its best features. The strategies and procedures you choose should be customized for your unique dataset and the insights you are looking to gain. You can try the different approaches to see which works best for you.

Takeaway

- Raw data is an ocean of valuable information and insights.
- It is common to be challenged by large datasets.
- The tools or techniques you use should depend on the nature of your data and your goal.

6

AI-DRIVEN DATA VISUALIZATION AND REPORTING

Importance of Data Visualization in Data Analytics

In the vast terrain of data engineering, where numbers hold sway, there exists an invaluable craft - data visualization. Think of it as the translator between data and understanding, and it's a language everyone can comprehend. Imagine you're handed a massive dataset, a sea of numbers and figures. How do you make sense of this numerical ocean? How do you unravel its secrets? The answer lies in wielding the tools of data visualization.

Data visualization transforms raw, impenetrable data into a canvas of colors, shapes, and forms that convey insights at a mere glance. It acts as the illuminator of data, making the complex comprehensible.

Now, why is visualization so essential in data engineering? Well, think about deciphering intricate patterns hidden within a labyrinth of data, it's a very stressful process. Data visualization, in this context, is your map, guiding you to the treasures in the data mine.

Data visualization uncovers concealed patterns and trends. Complex statistical analysis and calculations that might take hours become effortlessly evident. Moreover, it's a vigilant guard, capable of flagging outliers and anomalies, which often conceal valuable insights within.

Now, let's explore its pivotal role in data engineering. Data visualization is the universal language spoken not only by data scientists but also by analysts and decision-makers. It transcends language barriers, making intricate insights accessible to everyone, acting as a medium for telling stories, and devising predictions and strategies. Whether you're a data scientist exploring intricate datasets or a business analyst deciphering market trends, these visualization tools are your trusted companions in the world of data engineering.

Exploring Data Visualization Techniques and Tools

Let's explore the vast toolbox of data visualization.

Charts and Graphs: Think of bar charts, line graphs, and pie charts as the fundamental brushes in your toolkit. They're excellent for showcasing trends, comparisons, and distributions. A bar chart can vividly represent sales figures across different regions, highlighting the top performers.

Heatmaps: If you need to highlight patterns or variations, heatmaps are your go-to tool. Imagine analyzing patient data in healthcare. A heatmap can swiftly reveal areas with higher recovery rates, guiding decisions on resource allocation.

Interactive Dashboards:Imagine having all your visualizations neatly organized on a single screen, ready to convey a holistic story, that's what the dashboard offers. Tools like Tableau and Power BI empower users to explore data on their own. They combine different visualizations to provide a comprehensive overview.

Geospatial Visualizations: For projects involving geographic data, tools like GIS (Geographic Information Systems) steal the spotlight. They let you map out data, revealing geographical trends. For example, you can visualize COVID-19 spread by region using GIS tools.

Word Clouds: If your data includes text, word clouds can be a creative tool. They emphasize the frequency of specific terms. In a sentiment analysis project, a word cloud can make positive and negative sentiments pop out instantly.

Infographics: These are like intricate paintings. They weave together various visual elements—charts, icons, and text—to tell a story concisely. In business reports, an infographic can convey complex information in a reader-friendly format.

Selecting the right tool is a strategic decision, you must select your visualization tool based on data characteristics and the target audience. If for instance, you're working on a financial report, it's better to opt for interactive dashboards to allow stakeholders to explore financial data freely.

In healthcare, where patient outcomes are the focus, you could use geospatial visualizations to show recovery rates across different regions. When choosing, you have to consider the functionality to build a visual narrative.

Leveraging AI for Interactive and Dynamic Visualizations

Imagine having visualizations that respond to your every query and interaction in real time. AI makes it possible. AI can turn your data visualizations into dynamic companions. By adapting to your interactions with the data, AI-powered visualizations enable you to focus on particular data points or filter the data based on your preferences. It's like having a personalized tour guide through the data landscape.

But AI's role doesn't stop there. It becomes your data connoisseur, your personal sommelier of visualizations. Think of it as a Netflix recommendation engine but for data insights. When you're lost in the sea of data, AI steps in with suggestions tailored to your needs. AI can analyze your past interactions with the data and recommend visualizations that are most relevant to your current quest. It's like having an AI co-pilot on your data journey.

Have you ever found yourself spending hours picking the right chart type for a dataset or laboring to create visuals that highlight key trends? AI can be your savior here, automating these tedious tasks. AI in data engineering isn't just about dynamic visuals; it's about streamlining the entire visualization process.

AI can analyze your dataset and make the call on the best chart type to represent it effectively. It can even generate a series of visualizations that illuminate the most critical data trends, freeing you to focus on the true artistry of data interpretation and decision-making. It's like having an AI assistant that takes care of the mundane, leaving you with the meaningful.

Personalization

AI is all about personalization. Just as Netflix knows what shows to recommend based on your viewing history, AI can tailor visualizations to your preferences. Using the data you interact to create visualizations that are tailored to your requirements and interests.

Accessibility for All

Inclusivity is a core principle of AI-driven data visualization. AI can enhance accessibility for individuals with different abilities. For instance, AI can generate text descriptions of visualizations, ensuring that those with visual impairments can access the insights. It's like providing an audio commentary for a movie, but for data visualizations.

As you can see, the age of static and uninspiring data visualizations is fading into the past. AI has ushered in an era of interactive, dynamic, and personalized data storytelling.

Automated Report Generation with Natural Language Generation (NLG)

In the fast-paced world of data engineering, the demand for timely, insightful, and error-free reports is paramount. Here, we delve into the practicality of Natural Language Generation (NLG) in automated report generation. NLG isn't just a buzzword; it's a transformative force that is revolutionizing how we harness data.

NLG, fueled by artificial intelligence, takes the complexity out of data by translating it into easily digestible narratives, reports, and dashboards. But why does it matter? For starters, it saves an invaluable resource: time. In a world where manual report generation can be laborious and error-prone, NLG automates the process. This liberates your skilled workforce to focus on high-impact tasks while elevating the caliber of your reports.

NLG is a subcategory of Natural Language Processing (NLP) that specializes in crafting human-readable text from structured or unstructured data. At its core, automated report generation with NLG is a time-saver. It erases the need for laborious manual report creation, providing a streamlined solution. But NLG offers more than just efficiency gains. It's the sentinel of report accuracy and currency. Imagine reports that are always up-to-date and free from human error.

The heart of NLG's practicality lies in its knack for converting data into plain language. The complex becomes comprehensible. This democratizes data access across your organization. Reports are no longer reserved for data scientists; they are open to everyone. This newfound accessibility fosters data-driven decision-making at all levels. Efficiency soars, accuracy becomes the standard, insights flourish, and decision-making becomes data-backed.

Automated report generation with NLG is a multi-faceted gem. It is your efficiency booster, releasing your team from repetitive tasks. It is your accuracy enhancer, ensuring reports are perpetually on point. It is your insight generator, unearthing hidden gems within your data. It is your decision-making catalyst, enabling informed choices rooted in reliable data.

NLG is your stalwart companion in data engineering. It is your bridge between raw data and actionable insights. It not only streamlines your data operations but also elevates your entire data strategy.

Designing Effective Dashboards for Actionable Insights

When it comes to data engineering, designing an effective dashboard is very important, as it offers a portal for actionable insights. Here are the steps involved:

Step 1: Define Purpose and Audience

Before you even touch a data visualization tool, understand the dashboard's purpose. What decisions should it facilitate? What are the requirements of the main users? Let's assume you're building a sales dashboard. Your purpose might be to improve sales strategy, and your audience could include sales managers, marketing teams, and executives.

Step 2: Choose the Right Data Sources

Your dashboard's effectiveness hinges on data quality and relevance. Pick data sources that are dependable, up-to-date, and suited to your goals. If you're dealing with vast datasets, consider leveraging data warehousing or data lakes for robust storage and retrieval.

Step 3: Data Collection and Processing

Now, collect and process your chosen data. This involves data extraction, transformation, and loading (ETL). Use tools like SQL, Python, or ETL platforms to clean, structure, and unify your data. Remember, the cleaner the data, the sharper the insights.

Step 4: Determine Key Metrics

Identify the vital metrics that align with your dashboard's purpose. For our sales dashboard, this could include total revenue, sales growth, top-selling products, and customer acquisition cost. These metrics will be your compass as you design your dashboard.

Step 5: Visualization Design

This is where your dashboard starts taking shape. Use visualization tools like Tableau, Power BI, or custom code libraries (e.g., D3.js) to create compelling visuals. Keep these principles in mind:

a. Clarity and Simplicity

- Choose clear fonts, colors, and icons.
- Avoid clutter; each visual should serve a purpose.
- Prioritize simplicity without sacrificing depth.

b. Consistency

- Maintain a consistent design language across visuals.
- Use the same color schemes and fonts throughout.

c. Interactivity

- Ensure users can interact with the data. Enable drill-downs for deeper insights.
- Interactive filters and slicers are invaluable.

d. Storytelling

- Craft a narrative with your visuals. Guide users through a logical flow.
- Use annotations and text to explain insights.

Step 6: Actionable Insights

Remember, the ultimate goal is to empower action. Make sure your dashboard doesn't just display data; it nudges users to make informed decisions. In our sales dashboard, this could involve highlighting underperforming products or indicating regions with untapped potential.

Step 7: Usability and Accessibility

Usability is paramount. Arrange visuals logically, keeping the most critical information at the forefront. Employ intuitive layouts that make navigation effortless. Consider accessibility standards to accommodate users with disabilities. Ensure text alternatives for visuals and a logical tab order for screen readers.

Step 8: Testing and Iteration

Before rolling out your dashboard, rigorously test it. Ensure that data updates work seamlessly. Gather feedback from potential users to identify pain points and areas for improvement. Dashboards are living entities; they should evolve with changing requirements.

Step 9: Deployment and Training

Finally, deploy your dashboard to your intended users. Provide training and documentation if necessary. Remember that user adoption is critical; users should feel confident navigating and deriving insights from the dashboard.

Step 10: Ongoing Maintenance

Your dashboard isn't a one-time project. It requires continuous care. Regularly update data sources, verify visualizations, and respond to user feedback. By doing so, your dashboard remains a reliable compass in the ever-changing data landscape.

When done right, a well-crafted dashboard becomes a compass, guiding decision-makers toward success in an increasingly data-driven world.

Takeaway

- Data visualization helps non-technical teams make sense of data.
- It's not just about pretty charts; it's about insights that respond to your needs.
- NLG is the sentinel for report currency and accuracy.

PART III

ADVANCED APPLICATIONS AND FUTURE PERSPECTIVES

Advanced analytics might sound like a lot of work, but a lot of us don't like things to just end at data processing, especially me. After preparing the data for analysis, I like being involved in the analytic process, and it gives me great joy every time this process goes smoothly because it lets me know that I did a very good job with the cleaning. In this next part, you'll learn enough to get you ready enough to tackle complex data challenges.

But that's not all we'll be going through in this part. One thing that can affect the foundation of your data engineering journey is ethics. Unethical data usage can cause problems for your data processing journey, and to avoid this, we'll look at ethical data practices and data quality management. After that, all that's left to do is to practice, practice, and practice, after all, experience makes expertise.

7

______

ADVANCED ANALYTICS WITH AI

Introduction to Advanced Analytics and Predictive Modeling

Advanced Analytics and Predictive Modeling are exciting fields in the realm of data engineering, and they offer powerful ways to extract insights and make informed decisions based on data (Franks, 2012).

Advanced analytics is a comprehensive strategy that includes a range of data analysis methods (Bose, 2009). It delves further into more complicated ground than descriptive analytics does, answering more complex "what happened" queries. Advanced analytics answers questions like "why did it happen" and "what might happen in the future." It takes historical data, applies statistical, machine learning, and AI techniques, and uncovers patterns and correlations that might not be immediately apparent.

Predictive modeling, a subset of advanced analytics conjures up predictions about future events based on historical data, it uses statistical modeling, data mining methods, and machine learning (Kolokuri, 2023).

Imagine you're a hospital administrator, and you want to predict patient admissions in the upcoming months to allocate resources efficiently. You gather historical admission data, including factors like seasonality, public events, and previous admission rates. Now, predictive modeling steps in. It builds a model that can forecast future admissions based on these historical patterns.

Types of Predictive Models

1. Regression Models: These are your classic predictive models. A regression model predicts a numerical value depending on data features.
2. Classification Models: When you need to classify data, like identifying whether an email is spam or not, you turn to classification models.
3. Time Series Models: These models specialize in predicting future values based on past data points that are collected over time. Think stock prices, weather forecasts, or even website traffic.
4. Clustering Models: Clustering models are useful for grouping comparable data points. They discover hidden structures in your data, making analysis easier.
5. Recommendation Models: Ever wondered how Netflix suggests movies you might like? That's the work of recommendation models. They predict what you might be interested in based on your past behavior and that of similar users.

We need advanced analytics and predictive modeling because we as data engineers are in charge of data collection, storage, and processing. We're like the foundation for advanced analytics and predictive modeling, especially since these analytical approaches would be ineffective without high-quality, well-organized data.

In the data engineering world, you'll often hear terms like databases, data warehouses, and data lakes. These are the tools data engineers use to store and manage the data. Advanced analytics and predictive modeling are your secret weapons for uncovering insights and predicting future trends from data.

Leveraging AI for Exploratory Data Analysis (EDA)

EDA is your first step in any data science adventure (Larose & Larose, 2019). It prepares you for the process, allowing you to get cozy with your data, like meeting a new friend. You can identify any quirks or oddities, spot potential issues, and begin forming hypotheses about what the data might reveal.

There's a toolbox of techniques at your disposal during EDA, but these are the classics:

Data Visualization: You create colorful charts, graphs, and visual wonders to unveil your data's distribution, patterns, and outliers.

Descriptive Statistics: They spin tales of the data's central tendencies, spreads, and distributions using mean, median, and standard deviation.

Hypothesis Testing: For testing statistical hypotheses about your dataset, like whether the mean of a particular variable is different from a certain value.

In the grand scheme of data analysis, EDA is your starting point, and it comes before building those complex models, before diving into deep statistical analyses.

During EDA, you accomplish three key tasks:

Getting to Know the Data: This is where you become acquainted with the data's quirks. You'll learn about its distribution, spot outliers that might be errors or genuinely interesting observations, and uncover if any crucial information is missing.

Identifying Patterns and Trends: EDA helps you grasp the relationships between different variables. You can find correlations, understand how one variable might affect another, and reveal trends that might otherwise go unnoticed.

Formulating Hypotheses: EDA prompts you to develop hypotheses about what's happening in your data. These hypotheses guide your further investigations and might lead to exciting discoveries.

Since data engineers are the architects who design the grand library where all this data resides. They build the infrastructure—databases, data warehouses, data lakes—that data scientists and analysts rely on. Data analysts need a clean, well-structured dataset to paint their data stories, and we provide them with it.

The Process of EDA

Now, let's break down the process of EDA into a more structured approach:

1. Data Collection: Begin by gathering your data. It could be from databases, spreadsheets, or even web scraping.
2. Data Cleaning: Cleanse the data by addressing missing values, outliers, and errors. This step ensures your

analysis is based on solid ground.

3. Data Exploration: Dive into the data. Create visualizations, calculate summary statistics, and explore patterns. This is where EDA really shines.
4. Hypothesis Testing: If you have specific questions or theories, test them. Use statistical methods to confirm or refute your hypotheses.
5. Insights and Reporting: Finally, present your findings. Tell the data's story. Visualize your insights, share your discoveries, and make recommendations.

In a world flooded with data, EDA helps you navigate the data landscape, uncover treasures, and ultimately makes you a data-driven decision-maker.

Machine Learning Algorithms for Classification and Regression

With Machine Learning (ML) algorithms, we unlock the power to make predictions and draw insights from data (Raschka, 2019).

Classification algorithms are like the super-efficient sorting machines of the ML world. They take data and predict discrete values like "Yes" or "No," "Spam" or "Not Spam." It's the best tool for tasks like identifying spam emails, speech recognition, or even spotting cancer cells. It can be classified into:

Binary Classifiers: They sort between two variables. For instance, telling whether an email is spam or not, or determining if a cell is cancerous.

Multi-class Classifiers: These are the multitaskers, sorting data into multiple categories.

Classification Tools

Logistic Regression: Logistic Regression helps make decisions by considering the probability of an event occurring. It's perfect for binary decisions, like determining if an email is spam or not.

Decision Trees: Decision Trees piece together evidence by asking a series of questions, leading to a final verdict. These trees are incredibly versatile, suitable for both classification and regression tasks. Their knack for simplifying complex decisions makes them valuable allies in fields like medical diagnosis or customer churn prediction.

Random Forest: By combining the opinions of many trees, it achieves robustness and accuracy, reducing overfitting. Random Forest excels in tasks such as image classification, where it can distinguish between various objects in a picture.

Support Vector Machines (SVM): SVM is the master of boundary creation. It finds the most optimal line or curve that separates different classes of data. SVM is effective in applications like text categorization and facial recognition.

K-Nearest Neighbors (K-NN): K-NN makes predictions based on the votes of its closest neighbors. K-NN is handy when dealing with recommendation systems or identifying similar items in e-commerce.

Naive Bayes: This tool is incredibly good at making decisions based on probabilities. It's like a weather forecaster predicting rain based on cloud cover, temperature, and humidity. Naive Bayes works well for text classification tasks like spam detection and sentiment analysis.

Regression Tools

Linear Regression: Linear Regression assumes that the relationship between variables is, well, linear. It fits a straight line through your data, making it great for tasks like predicting house prices based on factors like square footage.

Non-linear Regression: When data doesn't follow a straight path, this tool can adapt. It's ideal for modeling complex relationships, like predicting the growth of a plant over time.

Polynomial Regression: It extends linear regression by fitting a polynomial equation to the data, capturing more complex relationships.

Support Vector Regression (SVR): Similar to SVM in classification, it is used in regression tasks to find the optimal hyperplane for predicting numeric values.

These superheroes, each with their unique powers, come to your rescue when you need to tackle classification or regression challenges. Whether you're fighting email spam, making medical diagnoses, or forecasting stock prices, you can count on them to bring order to the chaos of data.

In essence, ML algorithms for classification and regression help you make sense of data. Whether you're deciding if an email is spam or forecasting the next big stock market move, these algorithms are your secret weapons. So while dealing with datasets, remember that these algorithms are here to help you uncover insights, make predictions, and transform data into knowledge.

Natural Language Processing (NLP) for Text Analytics

Everybody has at some point (probably while you were younger), wondered how computers can understand and interact with human languages like English, Spanish, or Chinese, and now we're going to discuss it fully. We're going to explore Natural Language Processing (NLP), a fascinating field that bridges the gap between computers and our words (Raaijmakers, 2022).

To kick things off, let's clarify a few terms that people use interchangeably, a lot: Text mining, text analytics, and NLP. Text mining involves extracting patterns and trends from unstructured text data, like finding keywords in a massive collection of articles. Text analytics is the broader concept that includes text mining, along with tasks such as sentiment analysis and topic modeling. Now, NLP, or Natural is a subfield of computer science that helps computers understand the meaning behind words, phrases, and sentences.

NLP isn't just a buzzword; it's a powerhouse of techniques that have super abilities. NLP helps your computer to read and comprehend text just like you do. It's used for tasks that involve understanding the nuances of human language.

Roles of NLP

Sentiment Analysis: NLP helps determine the emotional tone of the text, classifying it as positive, negative, or neutral.

Topic Modeling: NLP can identify the main topics discussed in a vast collection of text. It's like having a librarian who can sort books into genres without reading them.

Named Entity Recognition: Imagine scanning a news article and instantly knowing which names are of people, places, or organizations. NLP does just that, it identifies and classifies named entities in text.

Text Summarization: Reading lengthy documents can be time-consuming. NLP comes to the rescue by generating concise and informative summaries. It's like having a robot assistant who can skim through books and provide you with the juicy bits.

Machine Translation: NLP isn't bound by language barriers. It can translate text from one language to another.

NLP isn't just about these tasks; it's a vital field for our data-driven world. NLP approaches are becoming increasingly relevant as more text data is being generated, they help make sense of the huge amounts of unstructured text data available, ranging from social media posts to medical records.

Step-by-Step Process of Text Analysis with NLP

Step 1: Data Collection and Preparation

Your NLP journey begins with data. Gather the text data you want to analyze. This could be customer reviews, news articles, or social media posts. Ensure the data is in a format that NLP tools can handle.

Step 2: Data Preprocessing

Text data can be messy with punctuation, special characters, and various forms of words (e.g., "run," "ran," "running"). Clean the data by removing noise, converting text to lowercase, and stemming or lemmatizing words to reduce them to their base form.

Step 3: Tokenization

Tokenization is like breaking a sentence into individual words or tokens. It's a crucial step to analyze text effectively. Imagine it as splitting a puzzle into pieces so that you can examine each one.

Step 4: Removal of Stop Words

In most text analysis tasks, common words, known as "stop words", like "the," "and," or "in" don't carry much meaning and can be removed. This step reduces the dimensionality of your data.

Step 5: Feature Extraction

Now, you need to convert text into numerical features that machine learning algorithms can understand. Techniques like TF-IDF (Term Frequency-Inverse Document Frequency) or word embeddings like Word2Vec can be incredibly helpful here.

Step 6: Choose Your NLP Task

Based on your goals, decide which NLP task you want to perform. Is it sentiment analysis, topic modeling, named entity recognition, text summarization, or machine translation? Each task requires specific techniques and tools.

Step 7: Model Selection

Select an appropriate NLP model or algorithm for your task. For example, for sentiment analysis, you might choose a pre-trained model like BERT or train a custom model with your data.

Step 8: Training and Evaluation

If needed, train your model using labeled data. Evaluate its performance using metrics relevant to your task, such as accuracy, precision, recall, or F1-score.

Step 9: Fine-tuning and Optimization

Refine your model by fine-tuning hyperparameters or exploring different architectures. This step is crucial for achieving the best results.

Step 10: Deployment and Scaling

Once your NLP model is ready, deploy it in your desired environment. It could be a web application, a chatbot, or an automated data analysis pipeline. Ensure it can scale to handle large volumes of text data.

Step 11: Continuous Monitoring and Improvement

NLP models require ongoing maintenance. Monitor their performance, gather user feedback, and retrain them periodically to adapt to changing language patterns.

NLP is a dynamic field, and there are always new techniques and tools emerging. Stay curious and keep exploring. As you master NLP for text analytics, you'll unlock powerful insights hidden within the vast sea of textual information.

AI-Powered Recommendation Systems and Personalization

I was online shopping recently, scrolling through eBay when some gadgets popped up, and I'm sure you've experienced this before as well when a list of products will suddenly appear, and they are usually tailored precisely to your preferences. This is a result of AI-powered recommendation systems.

Recommendation systems collect user data, such as browsing history, purchase, history, or even demographic information, after which AI steps in to make sense of the data, giving recommendation systems the ability to predict what a user might like.

One commonly used technique is collaborative filtering. It works by finding patterns in user behavior and matching users with similar preferences. For instance, if you and another user have both purchased similar books in the past, the system may recommend a book that the other user enjoyed but you haven't yet discovered.

Another approach is content-based filtering, which recommends items based on their attributes and descriptions. If you've been searching for running shoes, the system might suggest other running-related gear.

To make these recommendations, recommendation systems employ powerful machine learning algorithms. These algorithms continuously learn and adapt, ensuring that recommendations remain relevant over time.

One key concept in machine learning for recommendations is the idea of feature extraction. Features are characteristics that define an item or a user's preferences. For a movie recommendation system, features could include genre, director, and user ratings. By analyzing these features, the AI can make intelligent predictions.

Personalization is where recommendation systems truly shine. By understanding your unique preferences, these systems can curate a shopping experience that feels tailor-made just for you. This personal touch not only increases user satisfaction but also drives sales and customer loyalty.

Challenges and Ethical Considerations

As we embrace the marvels of AI-powered personalization, it's essential to address some critical challenges. There's the issue of the "filter bubble," where users only view content that aligns with their existing beliefs and preferences. This can limit diversity and information exposure.

Furthermore, privacy concerns arise when collecting and analyzing user data. Balancing personalization and user privacy is an ongoing challenge.

Building AI-Powered Recommendation Systems

Now that we've unveiled the mysteries behind recommendation systems, let's take a peek at how these systems are crafted.

Building recommendation systems involves a mix of data engineering and AI of course.

Data Collection and Preprocessing

First and foremost, we data engineers play a pivotal role in collecting and preprocessing the data that fuels recommendation systems. This data often includes user behavior logs, product information, and user profiles. And the data must be clean, structured, and ready for analysis. In our quest for personalization, remember that quality data is the lifeblood of AI. Without it, even the most advanced algorithms would falter.

Selecting the Right Algorithms

Choosing the right recommendation algorithm is like selecting the perfect tool for the job. You have to choose between collaborative filtering, content-based filtering, and hybrid models which all have their strengths and weaknesses. Machine learning libraries like TensorFlow and scikit-learn offer a treasure trove of algorithms for building recommendation systems. As data engineers, you'll need to evaluate which approach aligns best with your specific use case.

Training and Fine-Tuning

Once the algorithm is selected, the magic begins with training. Machine learning models require extensive training on historical data to understand user preferences accurately. This phase involves tweaking hyperparameters and optimizing the model for performance.

Real-Time Recommendations

At this point, you might need to collaborate with data scientists and software engineers to deploy recommendation models that can deliver suggestions instantly, as users navigate a platform.

Evaluation and A/B Testing

Building recommendation systems isn't a one-and-done task. Continuous evaluation is essential to ensure that recommendations remain effective and engaging. A/B testing allows you to compare different recommendation strategies and fine-tune them for better performance.

As technology advances, the future of AI-powered personalization looks promising. Machine learning models are becoming more sophisticated, and AI is branching into areas like natural language processing, enabling more nuanced and context-aware recommendations.

Imagine a future where recommendation systems not only know what products you might like but also understand your mood and suggest movies or music accordingly. The possibilities are boundless. And the best part? As a data engineer, the power to create remarkable experiences and drive innovation lies in your hands.

Text Mining and Sentiment Analysis

Imagine having a massive pile of unstructured text data—articles, reviews, social media posts, you name it (Cohen & Hunter, 2008). Text mining is the process that turns this chaos into knowledge. It's like deciphering a secret code hidden in the words. This process extracts valuable patterns, trends, and relationships from text data. Think of it as sorting through a library of books, finding keywords, and organizing them neatly.

Sentiment analysis, a subfield of text mining, is all about understanding the sentiment or tone of text data, which could be positive, negative, or neutral. Text mining and sentiment analysis work hand in hand. They're like the dynamic duo of data analysis.

Text Mining + Sentiment Analysis: Let's say you have a mountain of customer reviews about a new product. Text mining swoops in to organize the data, making sense of it all. It identifies those reviews and extracts their essence. Then, sentiment analysis steps in to reveal the feelings hidden in those words. Positive? Negative? Neutral? You name it! Now, you have insights into what customers love and loathe about your product. But it's not only for e-commerce, it plays a role in other areas, such as:

Customer Feedback Analysis: Businesses want to know what their customers are saying. By analyzing customer reviews, comments, and surveys, you can provide invaluable insights into customer satisfaction.

Market Research: Want to know the latest trends or what people are saying about your competitors? Text mining and sentiment analysis can sift through vast amounts of data to give you the answers.

Social Media Monitoring: With billions of social media posts daily, companies need to keep an eye on their brand mentions. These tools can help you track sentiment in real time.

Brand Reputation Management: Protecting a brand's reputation is crucial. Detecting negative sentiment early can help avert PR disasters.

Product Development: Feedback from users can shape your product roadmap. These techniques can identify what features are loved or loathed.

Risk Assessment: In the financial sector, analyzing news and social media sentiment can provide early warning signs of market trends or potential risks.

Building a text mining and sentiment analysis system using 'R':

Step 1: Install R and RStudio

Step 2: Install Required Packages

Open RStudio and install the necessary packages for text mining and sentiment analysis

Step 3: Load and Prepare Your Text Data

Import your text data into R. You can use various formats like CSV, and TXT, or scrape data from the web using packages like 'rvest' or 'httr'. Then preprocess the text data by removing special characters, and numbers, and converting text to lowercase

Step 4: Create a Term-Document Matrix

Now, create a term-document matrix (TDM) that represents the frequency of terms (words) in the text data

Step 5: Perform Sentiment Analysis

Utilize the 'tm.plugin.sentiment' package for sentiment analysis. You might need to provide a sentiment lexicon or dictionary depending on your analysis needs.

Step 6: Analyze and Visualize Sentiment

Now, you have sentiment scores for your text data. You can analyze and visualize the sentiment distribution:

Step 7: Interpret the Results

Interpret the results based on the sentiment scores. You can categorize text as positive, negative, or neutral depending on your sentiment analysis goals.

Step 8: Refine and Iterate

Text mining and sentiment analysis are iterative processes. You may need to refine your preprocessing steps, sentiment lexicon, or analysis approach based on your results.

Step 9: Deploy and Automate

If you plan to use this analysis regularly, consider creating a function or script for automation. This makes it easier to apply your text mining and sentiment analysis to new data.

Step 10: Share Insights

Finally, share your insights with stakeholders. Visualization and reports can help communicate your findings effectively.

Remember, text mining and sentiment analysis are versatile tools. You can apply them to various domains like customer feedback, social media monitoring, and market research. The key is to adapt the process to your specific data and analysis goals.

So, the next time you see a brand responding to customer feedback promptly or a company launching a product that feels tailor-made for you, remember the magic of text mining and sentiment analysis. They're not only about numbers and data, but also understanding people to make data-driven decisions that better life for us all.

Visual Analytics and Data Storytelling Using AI-Driven Tools

Have you ever been captivated by a compelling story? Well, I'm about to introduce you to a world where data becomes a storyteller, and it's all thanks to the Data Engineers (that includes you of course).

In a grand library filled with books of endless information, Data Engineers as the librarians, meticulously collect, clean, and organize these books (data) to make them accessible to everyone. In the realm of Data Storytelling, Data Engineers play a critical role, and we are the foundation upon which data storytelling stands tall. We gather, scrub it clean, and prepare data for analysis, ensuring it's ready for the spotlight.

We are also in charge of crafting the infrastructure—data warehouses, data lakes, and data pipelines, that lets data flow seamlessly.

But this isn't a solo job. Data Engineers collaborate closely with Data Scientists to create and deploy AI-powered models. These models have the remarkable ability to automate data analysis and storytelling tasks. It's like having a co-author who knows the story's essence, helping craft narratives that resonate with the audience.

Data Storytelling

Now, let's talk about Data Storytelling itself. Think of it as crafting a tale from the library we mentioned earlier. Data Engineers provide the foundation, but it's the data scientists and business users who transform this data into captivating narratives.

Data scientists rely on your well-organized data playbook to work their analytical magic, deploying machine learning models to extract useful insights from the data.

Imagine analyzing customer behavior data to uncover trends or deciphering market data to predict future trends. These insights build your story, and they can help you improve your business. It allows business users to harness the power of data and make informed decisions.

AI-driven tools and techniques, including machine learning models, add a layer of enchantment to this storytelling. They help sift through mountains of data, extracting the juiciest bits. AI understands the data's language and translates it into human-friendly insights.

You can also use AI-driven tools to explore data, understand customer sentiments, and predict future trends. Building the bridges and pathways for others to access and interpret data.

Visual Analytics and Data Storytelling with AI-driven tools are changing the way we interact with data. It's a tale of collaboration, where Data Engineers, Data Scientists, and business users work hand in hand to create narratives that drive success.

Anomaly Detection and Outlier Analysis Using AI

Anomalies are usually different, they are data points that stand out like a beacon- outliers, a peculiarity in the data that defies the norm.

Anomalies can come in various forms, from fraudulent transactions in financial data to defective components in manufacturing processes. The task at hand? Detecting these anomalies hidden within the vast sea of data. Here's where AI comes to our aid.

Machine Learning Methods for Anomaly Detection

1. Unsupervised Learning Algorithms

These are like detectives without prior knowledge, sifting through data to find peculiarities. Imagine clustering techniques that group similar data points and consider the outliers as anomalies.

2. Supervised Learning Methods

In this scenario, the AI detective has prior knowledge. It's trained on historical data and can differentiate between normal and anomalous patterns. This method is particularly useful in fraud detection.

3. Semi-Supervised Learning

Here, AI detectives work with limited labeled data but can still identify anomalies with a fair degree of accuracy. It's a bit like having some clues but not the full story.

4. Deep Learning and Neural Networks

These detectives are like the Sherlock Holmes of AI, capable of uncovering complex anomalies hidden within intricate data structures. They excel in image and text analysis, where anomalies can be disguised amidst vast information.

5. Hybrid Approaches

Much like a seasoned investigator who uses various tools and strategies, hybrid methods combine the strengths of different AI approaches to detect anomalies in multifaceted scenarios.

Types of Anomalies

Point Anomalies: These are solitary deviants, individual data points that sharply contrast with the rest.

Contextual Anomalies: Imagine data behaving like a chameleon, seemingly normal in one context but entirely bizarre in another. These anomalies change their appearance based on the situation.

Collective Anomalies: These mischievous anomalies are elusive, requiring a collective view of data over time to uncover. They might not stand out individually but disrupt patterns when examined collectively.

Whether you're seeking anomalies in financial transactions, outliers in customer behavior, or irregularities in sensor data, remember that AI is a tool to want to have in handy. With AI by your side, you can confidently chart the depths of data mysteries, revealing the treasures of insights hidden beneath.

Takeaway

- EDA prepares you for a successful data processing journey by acquainting you with the data.
- Machine learning algorithms help you uncover insights, make predictions, and transform data into knowledge.
- Quality data is the lifeblood of AI.
- Data engineers lay the foundation for data storytelling.

8

AI-POWERED DATA GOVERNANCE AND COMPLIANCE

Understanding Data Governance and Regulatory Compliance

Data governance is similar to the compass that guides our journey. It's the collection of processes, policies, standards, and structures that ensure data is managed properly within an organization (Harrison et al, 2019).

Data governance covers everything, every process, from data collection, to storage, usage, and even how it is governed. Data governance relies on the people, processes, and technologies that create, use, store, share, and govern data.

Moving on to Regulatory compliance, this means ensuring that an organization's activities align with all applicable laws and regulations. This includes data protection laws like the General Data Protection Regulation (GDPR) and the California Consumer Privacy Act (CCPA) (Dove, 2018).

Data governance and regulatory compliance are like two sides of the same coin. Data governance provides the framework to manage data transparently, accountably, and securely, which is vital for compliance. In essence, they're our navigation tools, helping us avoid the treacherous rocks of legal issues.

Let's delve into some of the most prominent data protection laws:

1. General Data Protection Regulation (GDPR)

Enforced by the European Union (EU), the GDPR is a comprehensive regulation designed to protect the personal data of EU citizens. It became effective on May 25, 2018 (Miglico, 2018).

<u>Key Provisions</u>:

- Data Subject Rights: GDPR grants individuals rights over their personal data, including the right to access, correct, delete, or port their data.
- Data Protection Officers (DPOs): Some organizations must appoint DPOs to oversee data protection efforts.
- Data Breach Notification: Organizations must report data breaches to authorities and affected individuals within specific timeframes.
- Privacy by Design: Organizations must embed privacy considerations in the design and implementation of systems and processes.
- Fines: GDPR introduces substantial fines for non-compliance, potentially reaching up to €20 million or 4% of a company's global annual revenue.

2. California Consumer Privacy Act (CCPA)

The CCPA is a state-level data protection law in California, effective from January 1, 2020. It provides Californian consumers with more control over their personal information (Harding et al, 2019).

<u>Key Provisions</u>:

- Right to Know: Consumers have the right to know what personal information businesses collect about them and how it's used.
- Right to Delete: Consumers can request the deletion of their personal data.
- Right to Opt-Out: Consumers can opt out of selling their personal information.
- Non-Discrimination: Businesses can't discriminate against consumers who exercise their rights under CCPA.
- Data Security: Businesses must implement reasonable security measures to protect consumer data.
- CCPA applies to businesses that meet specific criteria, including those with annual gross revenues exceeding $25 million.

3. HIPAA (Health Insurance Portability and Accountability Act)

HIPAA is a U.S. federal law that regulates the use and disclosure of individuals' protected health information (PHI). It applies to healthcare providers, insurers, and their business associates (Hansen, 1997).

<u>Key Provisions</u>:

- Privacy Rule: Sets standards for the use and disclosure of PHI.
- Security Rule: Requires safeguarding electronic PHI.

- Breach Notification Rule: Mandates the reporting of breaches involving PHI.
- HIPAA ensures the confidentiality, integrity, and availability of PHI.

These laws are put in place to protect folks' personal data. They have a significant impact on how organizations handle data, emphasizing the need for clear policies, data security measures, and mechanisms so that people can exercise their data rights.

Benefits of Data Governance for Compliance

1. Improved Data Quality and Accuracy

Data governance ensures that the data you rely on is trustworthy, reducing errors that could lead to compliance violations.

2. Increased Data Security

Data governance fortifies your data against unauthorized access, reducing the risk of data breaches.

3. Reduced Risk of Data Breaches

Compliance regulations often require safeguarding sensitive information. Data governance helps you maintain these protections effectively.

4. Efficient Compliance

Navigating the complex regulatory landscape can be challenging. Data governance provides a clear path, simplifying compliance processes.

5. Enhanced Decision-Making

High-quality, well-governed data provides better insights for informed decision-making, aligning your strategies with compliance requirements.

In conclusion, data governance and regulatory compliance are essentials for your data engineering journey. Data governance acts as your map, guiding how you handle data, while regulatory compliance keeps you safe from legal storms.

As you navigate through these waters, remember that data governance is not just about compliance; it's also about good data practices that lead to smoother sailing overall. So, embrace these tools, set your course, and chart a course toward successful data governance and regulatory compliance.

AI-based Data Quality Management and Metadata Management

Data quality management can be likened to the anchor of your data ship, keeping everything stable and reliable. With AI and ML are readily available to automate many tasks involved in data quality management (Frank et al, 2017).

With their help, tasks such as data profiling, anomaly detection, and data cleansing become a breeze. This means you, as a data professional, can free up your time for more strategic tasks, like improving data governance and ensuring data compliance.

AI can also assist in developing advanced data quality metrics and dashboards. These sophisticated tools allow organizations to understand the quality of their data better, helping them pinpoint areas that need improvement. You can think of these metrics and dashboards as your treasure map, guiding you to data quality gold.

Metadata, often referred to as data about data, is like your data logbook. It holds crucial information about the data's origin, meaning, and usage (Torre-Bastida et al, 2022).

Metadata management is all about collecting, organizing, and managing this precious information. AI lends a hand by automating tasks such as data discovery, data classification, and data lineage.

AI can help in crafting sophisticated metadata models too. These models are like a detailed map of your data world, allowing you to navigate the vast sea of information more effectively. And this can help organizations make better decisions based on their data, and ultimately help them be successful.

Benefits

Efficiency Boost: AI's automation reduces manual labor, allowing you to achieve more in less time.

Enhanced Data Quality: Automated data quality checks mean fewer errors and better data overall.

Regulatory Compliance Made Easier: With AI's assistance, ensuring compliance with data protection laws becomes a breeze.

Data Understanding: AI-driven metadata models help you understand your data's intricacies, leading to more informed decisions.

Strategic Focus: By automating routine tasks, AI lets you focus on the bigger picture, contributing to your organization's success.

By harnessing the power of AI, you can ensure that your data ship not only stays afloat but also sails confidently toward its destination.

Ensuring Data Ethics and Bias Mitigation in AI-driven Environments

Journeying through the ever-evolving landscape of data ethics and bias mitigation in AI-driven environments will teach you how to be guided by data ethics when wading through the many AI possibilities. Some of the principles that should be in your toolkit for ethical AI use include:

Transparency is important as it is crucial to be clear about how your AI systems work and make decisions. Transparency builds trust with users and uncovers potential biases hiding in the shadows. And organizations should be crystal clear about how their AI systems work and make decisions.

Another cardinal principle is accountability, organizations must be accountable for AI decisions. Clear policies and procedures should be in place to manage bias and ensure fair and responsible AI use. In essence, you become the steward of ethical AI.

Detecting and Mitigating Algorithmic Bias

Algorithmic bias can lead to disaster if one is not careful, creeping in through data used for training, design choices, or how the algorithm is used. It can lead to unfair outcomes, such as discriminatory loan denials or biased job recommendations. The best practices for detecting and mitigating algorithmic bias include:

Diverse Datasets: Using a diverse dataset to train your algorithm ensures it doesn't favor one group over another. Diversity keeps your AI on an unbiased course, by preventing bias from seeping into its models.

Transparency and Auditability: It involves keeping a logbook that ensures that your AI's decision-making process can be examined. When things go awry, you can trace back and correct the course.

Mitigation Techniques: Techniques such as oversampling or undersampling, are like adjusting sails for balance. They help ensure your AI doesn't tilt unfairly.

Continuous Monitoring: Monitoring over time is your compass, always checking if you're still on the right path.

Machine learning algorithms learn from data. If that data is biased, the algorithm becomes biased too. This can lead to unfair outcomes, much like a ship's course gone astray.

Navigating Ethical Concerns

Bias isn't our only concern and there are other ethical issues to deal with.

Privacy: It is very important to protect individuals' privacy. Privacy concerns arise when personal data is mishandled or exposed.

Explainability: Explainability demands that AI decisions can be understood and justified. Can you explain your AI's decisions?

Fairness: Fairness ensures AI doesn't favor any group unfairly. Ensure your AI treats everyone fairly. No favoritism allowed.

Transparency: This is the beacon to guide your way, shedding light on AI's inner workings.

Accountability: You're the captain; you're responsible for every decision made by your AI system. Organizations must have policies and procedures in place to manage bias and ensure AI systems are used responsibly.

Ensuring data ethics and mitigating bias in AI-driven environments is your ethical duty as a data engineer.

Data Cataloging and Data Lineage with AI

Data lineage, my friend, is tracking data from its source to its purpose. This is where we uncover how data transforms and where potential hazards like data quality issues or leaks lie hidden beneath the surface (Fernández, et al, 2014).

Now, data cataloging involves organizing and labeling your dataset (Eryurek et al, 2021). It ensures that all your precious data assets are neatly organized, easily discoverable, and understandable. Imagine being able to find your treasure effortlessly and knowing precisely what's inside each chest.

Generative AI, a powerful ally, breathes life into data catalogs. It crafts catalogs that are comprehensive and always up-to-date. Unlike traditional catalogs, it learns from the data itself. It's as if it possesses the skills of an experienced cartographer who can extract metadata automatically from our data treasures.

Moreover, AI isn't just creating basic lineage maps, it understands the complex relationships between data assets. With AI at the helm, we get lineage graphs that truly reflect these relationships, steering us away from treacherous data seas.

Practical Steps for Enhancing Data Cataloguing and Data Lineage Practices

Step 1: Embrace AI-Powered Tools

First, you need the right tools. Look for AI-powered data cataloging and lineage tools (like SQL) that fit your needs. You can save time and reduce the risk of errors by automating tasks with these tools.

Step 2: Data Profiling and Discovery

Begin with data profiling. AI can help you understand the nature of your data better by analyzing it and revealing hidden insights.

Step 3: AI-Enhanced Cataloging

Use AI to create comprehensive data catalogs. These catalogs should automatically extract metadata, making it easier for your crew (your team) to discover and use data effectively.

Step 4: Automate Lineage Tracking

AI can automatically track data lineage. It identifies relationships between data assets and generates clear, concise lineage graphs. This helps everyone on board understand how data flows through your systems.

Step 5: Continuous Monitoring

Continuously monitor your AI-enhanced catalog and lineage. Make adjustments as needed to ensure everything runs smoothly.

Step 6: Documentation and Training

Document your AI-augmented processes. Train your crew (team) on how to use these AI tools effectively. This ensures everyone can navigate the data seas with confidence.

In the ever-expanding realm of data engineering, AI serves as the North Star. It simplifies the complexities of data cataloging and data lineage, guiding us toward comprehensive, accurate, and efficient solutions.

AI-driven Data Governance Frameworks and Best Practices

Together, let's uncover how AI-driven data governance frameworks and best practices can make this journey more efficient, effective, and, dare I say, exciting. AI guides us through the intricate waters of data governance, automating tasks that once required significant human effort.

With AI by our side, we automate tasks like data profiling, data quality checks, and data lineage tracking. These once-tedious tasks become a breeze, improving the efficiency and effectiveness of our data governance efforts.

Mitigating Bias and Risk

One of the many benefits of AI is the ability to identify and mitigate bias in data (Norori et al, 2021). Bias can lead to unfair or discriminatory outcomes, especially when making decisions about people. Think of AI as the compass that points out potential biases hidden within our data. It helps us steer clear while ensuring fairness and transparency in our decisions.

Moreover, AI is our lookout, scanning the horizon for hidden risks in data governance. It can identify and mitigate risks that might elude the human eye. This is vital because data governance is all about managing risk, and AI is our guardian against unexpected storms.

Benefits of AI-Powered Tools in Data Governance

Increased Efficiency: These tools automate tasks such as data discovery and data classification. This automation frees up our time to focus on other priorities, making our journey smoother.

Improved Accuracy: AI-powered tools help us spot and address risks, such as data bias and potential data breaches. They're like our sharp-eyed lookout, ensuring the accuracy and integrity of our data.

Enhanced Compliance: AI ensures that our data governance practices align with regulations.

Best Practices for AI-Driven Data Governance

Define Clear Goals: Like setting the course, clearly define your goals and objectives for data governance. Know where you want to go.

Identify Data Assets: Recognize the data assets that need governance, and protect them.

Risk Assessment Framework: Develop a robust risk assessment framework, and it will help you navigate safely through potential hazards.

AI Automation: Implement AI-powered tools to automate tasks and identify risks.

Monitor and Evaluate: Keep a watchful eye on your data governance practices. Regularly evaluate their effectiveness and make adjustments as needed.

As we journey through the ever-evolving sea of data governance, remember that AI is your steadfast companion. It streamlines your efforts, mitigates risks, and ensures compliance. With AI by your side, data governance becomes smoother, more efficient, and full of promise.

Takeaway

- Data governance and compliance guide ethical data management and protect users' privacy.

- Harnessing AI helps you confidently sail your ship toward success.
- With ethical data usage, you're not just charting data courses; you're shaping the ethical future of AI.

CONCLUSION

For coming this far, I believe it's because you view this book as a portal to a future where data processing and analytics are transformed by the incredible power of Artificial Intelligence.

I can see you already standing at the edge of a vast data landscape, armed with the knowledge from each chapter of this book., now that you've learned how data engineering and AI work in harmony, and you're most likely ready to harness their potential.

At the beginning, I introduced you to the dynamic duo of Data Engineering and AI and their monumental impact on data processing and analytics, which has shown you the potential for AI to revolutionize the very core of data engineering. After which you were equipped with the tools to collect, validate, clean, and integrate data efficiently. Together we explored the evolution of data storage, and now you understand how AI can bolster data security and privacy while making retrieval a breeze.

At the second part, you learned how to be more efficient by letting AI shoulder the heavy lifting, automating workflows and optimizing real-time data analysis, and how to effortlessly extract valuable insights from data and engineer features. Next, we focused on turning data into captivating visuals, and also how to analyze data and take on complex data challenges.

Last, but most importantly, we discussed AI-powered Data Governance and Compliance. And I believe you've grasped the importance of ethical data practices, data quality management, and metadata, ensuring that your data empire stands on a solid foundation.

You've discovered how the synergy between data engineering and AI can supercharge your data endeavors. You've learned the art of efficient data collection, storage, transformation, and visualization, all while upholding data ethics and compliance. Armed with this knowledge, you're prepared to lead the charge in the data-driven world.

But remember, knowledge alone is just potential power. Now that you have all the tools, it's time to go out there and use them. Dive into your data projects with the vigor and confidence you've gained from this book. Put AI and data engineering to work, turning raw data into meaningful insights, actionable strategies, and innovative solutions.

If you've found this book enlightening and valuable, please consider leaving a review on Amazon. Your feedback will guide fellow data enthusiasts on their own journeys of discovery.

As you venture forth into the exciting world of Data Engineering and AI, remember this: You are the architect of data's future. Embrace the revolution, lead with integrity, and let your data-driven dreams soar. The world of possibilities is now yours to explore.

AFTERWORD

First and foremost, I want to express my heartfelt gratitude for choosing my book among countless others. Your decision to embark on this journey with me means the world, and I am truly honored to have you as a reader.

I would also like to congratulate you for making it to the end.

Before you part ways, would you be willing to share your thoughts and experiences by leaving a review on the platform? Your honest feedback not only helps other potential readers make informed decisions but also serves as a beacon of encouragement for independent authors like myself.

I eagerly look forward to hearing from you. Together, we can make a difference through the power of words.

>> Scan QR code to leave a review<<

BIBLIOGRAPHY

References

Fenwick, D., Daim, T. U., & Gerdsri, N. (2009). Value Driven Technology Road Mapping (VTRM) process integrating decision making and marketing tools: Case of Internet security technologies. Technological Forecasting and Social Change, 76(8), 1055-1077.

Pitt, A., & Britzman, D. (2003). Speculations on qualities of difficult knowledge in teaching and learning: An experiment in psychoanalytic research. Qualitative studies in education, 16(6), 755-776.

Najafabadi, M. M., Villanustre, F., Khoshgoftaar, T. M., Seliya, N., Wald, R., & Muharemagic, E. (2015). Deep learning applications and challenges in big data analytics. Journal of big data, 2(1), 1-21.

Diaz, O., Kushibar, K., Osuala, R., Linardos, A., Garrucho, L., Igual, L., ... & Lekadir, K. (2021). Data preparation for artificial intelligence in medical imaging: A comprehensive guide to open-access platforms and tools. Physica medica, 83, 25-37.

Carbone, P., Katsifodimos, A., Ewen, S., Markl, V., Haridi, S., & Tzoumas, K. (2015). Apache flink: Stream and batch processing in a single engine. The Bulletin of the Technical Committee on Data Engineering, 38(4).

Lin, J., & Ryaboy, D. (2013). Scaling big data mining infrastructure: the twitter experience. Acm SIGKDD Explorations Newsletter, 14(2), 6-19.

Sarker, I. H. (2021). Data science and analytics: an overview from data-driven smart computing, decision-making and applications perspective. SN Computer Science, 2(5), 377.

Janssen, M., Brous, P., Estevez, E., Barbosa, L. S., & Janowski, T. (2020). Data governance: Organizing data for trustworthy Artificial Intelligence. Government Information Quarterly, 37(3), 101493.

Ghazal, T. M., Hasan, M. K., Alshurideh, M. T., Alzoubi, H. M., Ahmad, M., Akbar, S. S., ... & Akour, I. A. (2021). IoT for smart cities: Machine learning approaches in smart healthcare—A review. Future Internet, 13(8), 218.

Berger, A. M., & Berger, C. R. (2004). Data mining as a tool for research and knowledge development in nursing. CIN: Computers, Informatics, Nursing, 22(3), 123-131.

Burgess, A., & Burgess, A. (2018). AI in Action. The Executive Guide to Artificial Intelligence: How to identify and implement applications for AI in your organization, 73-89.

Saxena, D., Raychoudhury, V., Suri, N., Becker, C., & Cao, J. (2016). Named data networking: a survey. Computer Science Review, 19, 15-55.

Pan, Y., & Zhang, L. (2021). Roles of artificial intelligence in construction engineering and management: A critical review and future trends. Automation in Construction, 122, 103517.

Stark, J. (2020). Digital transformation of industry. Springer International Publishing.

Buduma, N., Buduma, N., & Papa, J. (2022). Fundamentals of deep learning. "O'Reilly Media, Inc.".

McAdams, D. P. (2015). The art and science of personality development. Guilford Publications.

Cao, L. (2017). Data science: a comprehensive overview. ACM Computing Surveys (CSUR), 50(3), 1-42.

Laguna, M., & Marklund, J. (2018). Business process modeling, simulation and design. Chapman and Hall/CRC.

Zhou, L., Pan, S., Wang, J., & Vasilakos, A. V. (2017). Machine learning on big data: Opportunities and challenges. Neurocomputing, 237, 350-361.

Pine, B. J., & Gilmore, J. H. (2011). The experience economy. Harvard Business Press.

Marques, J. P., Meineke, J., Milovic, C., Bilgic, B., Chan, K. S., Hedouin, R., ... & Schweser, F. (2021). QSM reconstruction challenge 2.0: A realistic in silico head phantom for MRI data simulation and evaluation of susceptibility mapping procedures. Magnetic Resonance in Medicine, 86(1), 526-542.

Demirkan, H., & Delen, D. (2013). Leveraging the capabilities of service-oriented decision support systems: Putting analytics and big data in cloud. Decision Support Systems, 55(1), 412-421.

Damiani, A., Masciocchi, C., Lenkowicz, J., Capocchiano, N. D., Boldrini, L., Tagliaferri, L., ... & Valentini, V. (2021). Building an artificial intelligence laboratory based on real world data: the experience of gemelli generator. Frontiers in Computer Science, 3, 768266.

Howard, A. B. (2014). The art and science of data-driven journalism.

Hurwitz, J. S., Nugent, A., Halper, F., & Kaufman, M. (2013). Big data for dummies. John Wiley & Sons.

Simsion, G., & Witt, G. (2004). Data modeling essentials. Elsevier.

Komatineni, S., MacLean, D., & Hashimi, S. Y. (2012). Pro Android 4 (Vol. 1, pp. 519-521). Berkeley, CA: Apress.

29. Chapman, A. D. (2005). Principles of data quality. GBIF.

Rueden, C. T., Schindelin, J., Hiner, M. C., DeZonia, B. E., Walter, A. E., Arena, E. T., & Eliceiri, K. W. (2017). ImageJ2: ImageJ for the next generation of scientific image data. BMC bioinformatics, 18, 1-26.

McEwen, A., & Cassimally, H. (2013). Designing the internet of things. John Wiley & Sons.

Talha, M., Abou El Kalam, A., & Elmarzouqi, N. (2019). Big data: Trade-off between data quality and data security. Procedia Computer Science, 151, 916-922.

Wylde, V., Rawindaran, N., Lawrence, J., Balasubramanian, R., Prakash, E., Jayal, A., ... & Platts, J. (2022). Cybersecurity, data privacy and blockchain: a review. SN Computer Science, 3(2), 127.

Mayer-Schönberger, V., & Cukier, K. (2013). Big data: A revolution that will transform how we live, work, and think. Houghton Mifflin Harcourt.

2. Phillips-Wren, G., Iyer, L. S., Kulkarni, U., & Ariyachandra, T. (2015). Business analytics in the context of big data: A roadmap for research. Communications of the Association for Information Systems, 37(1), 23.

Nafea, I. T. (2018). Machine learning in educational technology. Machine learning-advanced techniques and emerging applications, 175-183.

Bergh, C., Benghiat, G., & Strod, E. (2019). The dataOps cookbook. DataKitchen Hqrs.

Dumas, M., La Rosa, M., Mendling, J., & Reijers, H. A. (2018). Fundamentals of business process management (Vol. 2). Heidelberg: Springer.

Friedman, E., & Tzoumas, K. (2016). Introduction to Apache Flink: stream processing for real time and beyond. " O'Reilly Media, Inc.".

Rabah, K. (2018). Convergence of AI, IoT, big data and blockchain: a review. The lake institute Journal, 1(1), 1-18.

Dong, L., & Zhang, J. (2021). Predicting polycyclic aromatic hydrocarbons in surface water by a multiscale feature extraction-based deep learning approach. Science of The Total Environment, 799, 149509.

Varsha, K. S., & Pai, M. L. (2020). Bharatanatyam Hand Mudra Classification Using SVM Classifier with HOG Feature Extraction. Innovations in Computer Science and Engineering: Proceedings of 7th ICICSE, 175-183.

Verdonck, T., Baesens, B., Óskarsdóttir, M., & vanden Broucke, S. (2021). Special issue on feature engineering editorial. Machine Learning, 1-12.

Anowar, F., Sadaoui, S., & Selim, B. (2021). Conceptual and empirical comparison of dimensionality reduction algorithms (pca, kpca, lda, mds, svd, lle, isomap, le, ica, t-sne). Computer Science Review, 40, 100378.

Laursen, R. A., & Alo, P. (2023). Transform Diabetes-Harnessing Transformer-Based Machine Learning and Layered Ensemble with Enhanced Training for Improved Glucose Prediction (Master's thesis, University of Agder).

Jonsson, P., & Wohlin, C. (2004, September). An evaluation of k-nearest neighbour imputation using likert data. In 10th International Symposium on Software Metrics, 2004. Proceedings. (pp. 108-118). IEEE.

Navada, A., Ansari, A. N., Patil, S., & Sonkamble, B. A. (2011, June). Overview of use of decision tree algorithms in machine learning. In 2011 IEEE control and system graduate research colloquium (pp. 37-42). IEEE.

Binte Ayaz, S. (2023). Lead Scoring with Machine Learning (Doctoral dissertation).

Irwin, B. W., Mahmoud, S., Whitehead, T. M., Conduit, G. J., & Segall, M. D. (2020).

Imputation versus prediction: applications in machine learning for drug discovery. Future Drug Discovery, 2(2), FDD38.

Mirza, B., Wang, W., Wang, J., Choi, H., Chung, N. C., & Ping, P. (2019). Machine learning and integrative analysis of biomedical big data. Genes, 10(2), 87.

Anderson, S. F. (2017). Technologies of vision: the war between data and images. MIT Press.

Theodorou, A., Wortham, R. H., & Bryson, J. J. (2016, April). Why is my robot behaving like that? Designing transparency for real time inspection of autonomous robots. In AISB workshop on principles of robotics. Sheffield, South Yorkshire, UK: Bath University Press, 2016.

Lotfi, F., Beheshti, A., Farhood, H., Pooshideh, M., Jamzad, M., & Beigy, H. (2023). Storytelling with Image Data: A Systematic Review and Comparative Analysis of Methods and Tools. Algorithms, 16(3), 135.

Harrison, T., F. Luna-Reyes, L., Pardo, T., De Paula, N., Najafabadi, M., & Palmer, J. (2019, June). The data firehose and AI in government: Why data management is a key to value and ethics. In Proceedings of the 20th annual international conference on digital government research (pp. 171-176).

Dove, E. S. (2018). The EU general data protection regulation: implications for international scientific research in the digital era. Journal of Law, Medicine & Ethics, 46(4), 1013-1030.

Miglicco, G. (2018). GDPR is here and it is time to get serious. Computer Fraud & Security, 2018(9), 9-12.

Harding, E. L., Vanto, J. J., Clark, R., Hannah Ji, L., & Ainsworth, S. C. (2019). Understanding the scope and impact of the california consumer privacy act of 2018. Journal of Data Protection & Privacy, 2(3), 234-253.

Hansen, E. (1997). HIPAA (Health Insurance Portability and Accountability Act) rules: federal and state enforcement. Medical Interface, 10(8), 96-8.

Frank, M., Roehrig, P., & Pring, B. (2017). What to do when machines do everything: How to get ahead in a world of ai, algorithms, bots, and big data. John Wiley & Sons.

Torre-Bastida, A. I., Gil, G., Miñón, R., & Díaz-de-Arcaya, J. (2022). Technological Perspective of Data Governance in Data Space Ecosystems. In Data Spaces: Design, Deployment and Future Directions (pp. 65-87). Cham: Springer International Publishing.

Fernández, A., del Río, S., López, V., Bawakid, A., del Jesus, M. J., Benítez, J. M., & Herrera, F. (2014). Big Data with Cloud Computing: an insight on the computing environment, MapReduce, and programming frameworks. Wiley Interdisciplinary Reviews: Data Mining and Knowledge Discovery, 4(5), 380-409.

Eryurek, E., Gilad, U., Lakshmanan, V., Kibunguchy-Grant, A., & Ashdown, J. (2021). Data Governance: The Definitive Guide. " O'Reilly Media, Inc.".

Norori, N., Hu, Q., Aellen, F. M., Faraci, F. D., & Tzovara, A. (2021). Addressing bias in big data and AI for health care: A call for open science. Patterns, 2(10).

Franks, B. (2012). Taming the big data tidal wave: Finding opportunities in huge data streams with advanced analytics. John Wiley & Sons.

Bose, R. (2009). Advanced analytics: opportunities and challenges. Industrial Management & Data Systems, 109(2), 155-172.

Kolukuluri, M., Devi, V. K., Tejaswini, S. S., & Anusha, K. (2023). Business Intelligence Using Data Mining Techniques And Predictive Analytics. Journal of Pharmaceutical Negative Results, 6923-6932.

Larose, C. D., & Larose, D. T. (2019). Data science using Python and R. John Wiley & Sons.

Raschka, S. (2015). Python machine learning. Packt publishing ltd.

Raaijmakers, S. (2022). Deep Learning for Natural Language Processing. Simon and Schuster.

Cohen, K. B., & Hunter, L. (2008). Getting started in text mining. PLoS computational biology, 4(1), e20.